JUDE

CONTENDING FOR THE FAITH IN TODAY'S CULTURE

JACKIE HILL PERRY

LifeWay Press®
Nashville, Tennessee

EDITORIAL TEAM, STUDENT MINISTRY PUBLISHING

Ben Trueblood
Director, Student Ministry

John Paul Basham
Manager,
Student Ministry
Publishing

Karen Daniel
Editorial Team Leader

Morgan Hawk
Content Editor

Jennifer Siao
Production Editor

Amy Lyon
Graphic Designer

Published by LifeWay Press® • © 2019 Jackie Hill Perry

ISBN: 978-1-5359-5144-9
Item: 005813849
Dewey decimal classification: 248.83
Subject heading: BIBLE. N.T. JUDE—STUDY AND
                 TEACHING/FAITH/EVANGELISTIC
                 WORK

To order additional copies of this resource, write LifeWay Church Resources Customer Service; One LifeWay Plaza; Nashville, TN 37234; FAX order to 615.251.5933; call toll-free 800.458.2772; email orderentry@lifeway.com; or order online at www.lifeway.com.

Printed in the United States of America.

Student Ministry Publishing, LifeWay Church Resources, One LifeWay Plaza, Nashville, TN 37234

Author is represented by Wolgemuth & Associates.

Table of
CONTENTS

ABOUT THE AUTHOR

JACKIE HILL PERRY is a Bible teacher, writer, and artist. She is the author of *Gay Girl, Good God: The Story of Who I Was, and Who God Has Always Been*. At home she is known as wife to Preston and mommy to Eden and Autumn.

HOW TO USE

Welcome to *Jude: Contending for the Faith in Today's Culture*!
I pray this study leads to boldness of faith and faithful study of
God's Word.

In each session, you'll find a group guide along with four sections
of personal study. If you are leading a group through this study,
check out the Leader Guide on pages 168-172.

IN THE BIBLE STUDY BOOK

WATCH

Watch the video for each session of the study, answering the
questions as you do. Continue answering the questions on this
page together as a group and discuss your answers.

PERSONAL STUDY

The following sections are for your personal study throughout the
week. There are four sections for each week (and a fifth section
on the last week of study). You can complete one section each
day or spread them out over multiple days. This study will require
you to dive deep into Scripture—take your time! This study will
also ask questions that are meant to provoke critical thinking and
personal worship. You may not have the answer to every question
and that's OK. The goal is to develop the skills to study God's
Word and apply the truth found in Scripture to our everyday lives.

LEADER GUIDE

If you are leading a group, the Leader Guide will walk you through
an optional session outline with additional discussion questions
and prompts for your group time.

INTRODUCTION

I first discovered Jude when I was a year into knowing Jesus and full of uncertainty about what that actually meant. I'd spent the majority of my Bible reading in the common books like John, Romans, and Psalms—all of the books Christians like to quote—and not once had I heard them make reference to Jude. I don't know how I didn't notice it myself, as if I didn't have to see it after skimming through 3 John and before tiptoeing toward Revelation. But when I did, I had no clue what I was getting myself into. As I read, the talk of angels being kept in chains and the devil arguing with an archangel over Moses' body was all too odd for me to even try to understand, but I kept going anyway trusting that God must have something to say to me in this strange little book. Eventually the words, "Now to him who is able to keep you from stumbling ..." stood up and looked me dead in the face. I didn't keep reading to the end of the sentence; I stayed there, staring at the words hoping they were true. For far too long in my Christian faith, I'd been afraid that my being kept was dependent upon the strength of my own hands, but according to Jude, it was to Him who was able, not me. It was unnerving that this book that I'd been ignoring for so long had a heaven-sent answer to my unsaid questions.

I think the Bible is like that, full of surprises. Every page, paragraph, sentence, and word has in it something God wants us to hear. And that's really the thing, it's that God has given us His Word so that we might know Him. Period. The stories and narratives are cool and all when taken at face value but when you dig into what's written and how it's pointing to the One for whom you were made, the words come alive. It's then able to unveil our hearts, readjust our minds, redirect our focus, anchor our feet, and strengthen our legs. Because Jude is God breathed (2 Tim. 3:16), it can do all of the above and so much more.

When I originally read Jude, the closing doxology is what stood out to me most, but after spending a significant amount of time in Jude in preparation for this study, I now see that this letter has so much to teach us about how to live in our current cultural climate as well. Jude's letter will not only teach you about God's mercy through Jesus Christ but it'll also challenge you to be merciful. It won't just provide wisdom on how to love those who are falling but it will also instruct you on how to remain standing. Unlike some of the more popular "Christian" books and approaches to ministry, Jude does not mince his words in the name of compassion. This letter is difficult to understand with themes that are quite uncomfortable at times but I'm grateful for it. Grateful that we serve a God, who through a man, was willing to say the difficult things if it meant we'd know and believe the truth. The truth might hurt sometimes but it's what sets us free. For that reason and more I'm excited (and I say that in the most melancholy introverted way possible) for you to study this small and yet glorious book. God has a lot to say, and I'm encouraged that you've made the commitment to listen.

THE BOOK OF JUDE

GREETING

Jude, a servant of Jesus Christ and brother of James,

To those who are called, beloved in God the Father and kept for Jesus Christ:

²May mercy, peace, and love be multiplied to you.

JUDGMENT ON FALSE TEACHERS

³Beloved, although I was very eager to write to you about our common salvation, I found it necessary to write appealing to you to contend for the faith that was once for all delivered to the saints. ⁴For certain people have crept in unnoticed who long ago were designated for this condemnation, ungodly people, who pervert the grace of our God into sensuality and deny our only Master and Lord, Jesus Christ.

⁵Now I want to remind you, although you once fully knew it, that Jesus, who saved a people out of the land of Egypt, afterward destroyed those who did not believe. ⁶And the angels who did not stay within their own position of authority, but left their proper dwelling, he has kept in eternal chains under gloomy darkness until the judgment of the great day—⁷just as Sodom and Gomorrah and the surrounding cities, which likewise indulged in sexual immorality and pursued unnatural desire, serve as an example by undergoing a punishment of eternal fire.

⁸Yet in like manner these people also, relying on their dreams, defile the flesh, reject authority, and blaspheme the glorious ones. ⁹But when the archangel Michael, contending with the devil, was disputing about the body of Moses, he did not presume to pronounce a blasphemous judgment, but said, "The Lord rebuke you." ¹⁰But these people blaspheme all that they do not understand, and they are destroyed by all that they, like unreasoning animals, understand instinctively. ¹¹Woe to them! For they walked in the way of Cain and abandoned themselves for the sake of gain to Balaam's error and perished in Korah's rebellion. ¹²These are hidden reefs

at your love feasts, as they feast with you without fear, shepherds feeding themselves; waterless clouds, swept along by winds; fruitless trees in late autumn, twice dead, uprooted; [13]wild waves of the sea, casting up the foam of their own shame; wandering stars, for whom the gloom of utter darkness has been reserved forever.

[14]It was also about these that Enoch, the seventh from Adam, prophesied, saying, "Behold, the Lord comes with ten thousands of his holy ones, [15]to execute judgment on all and to convict all the ungodly of all their deeds of ungodliness that they have committed in such an ungodly way, and of all the harsh things that ungodly sinners have spoken against him." [16]These are grumblers, malcontents, following their own sinful desires; they are loud-mouthed boasters, showing favoritism to gain advantage.

A CALL TO PERSEVERE

[17]But you must remember, beloved, the predictions of the apostles of our Lord Jesus Christ. [18]They said to you, "In the last time there will be scoffers, following their own ungodly passions." [19]It is these who cause divisions, worldly people, devoid of the Spirit. [20]But you, beloved, building yourselves up in your most holy faith and praying in the Holy Spirit, [21]keep yourselves in the love of God, waiting for the mercy of our Lord Jesus Christ that leads to eternal life. [22]And have mercy on those who doubt; [23]save others by snatching them out of the fire; to others show mercy with fear, hating even the garment stained by the flesh.

DOXOLOGY

[24]Now to him who is able to keep you from stumbling and to present you blameless before the presence of his glory with great joy, [25]to the only God, our Savior, through Jesus Christ our Lord, be glory, majesty, dominion, and authority, before all time and now and forever. Amen.

JUDE 1-2

As you watch the Week 1 video, answer the following questions:

- Who does Jude say that he is? Who is he writing to?
- What does Jackie say it means to bless someone? Who is the one to bless and keep them?
- What three things does Jude want his recipients to receive from God?
- How can we have an abounding love for others?

After watching the Week 1 video, discuss the following together as a group:

- Read all of Jude aloud.
- Look up and define any words you didn't recognize.
- We have already received mercy from God as His called, and we are to show the same mercy we have received. When have you felt God's mercy in your life?
- Why do you think we need to experience God's love in order to show love to others?

> JUDE, A SERVANT OF JESUS CHRIST AND BROTHER OF JAMES, TO THOSE WHO ARE CALLED, BELOVED IN GOD THE FATHER AND KEPT FOR JESUS CHRIST: ²MAY MERCY, PEACE, AND LOVE BE MULTIPLIED TO YOU.
>
> JUDE 1-2

At the beginning of each session, I'll have a few verses of Jude for you to read. Jot down a few of your initial observations of the verses, and then spend some time in prayer before beginning your personal study.

Don't skip this part. Observation is an imperative part of studying the Scriptures. This is where you'll get the chance to pay attention to the little things you're reading so you can figure out the big picture. This is where you get to interrogate the text. Ask it questions like "Why is this there?" "What does this mean?" "Isn't that a contradiction?" "Why is there a 'but' here instead of an 'or'?" "I've seen this word used a lot in one paragraph, I wonder why?" Then, turn your observations into a conversation with God, so you're actually asking God these questions and allowing Him, by His Spirit, to lead you to the answers.

Studying without observing is like trying to do your homework without reading the instructions. Each week, I want you to pray for God to show you Himself through His Word. Pray that He would give you understanding of the Scriptures and help you to apply what you are learning.

DAY 1

Read over Jude.

OK, now that you've read it once, read it again.

What's your first reaction to what you've read?

What do you sense is the theme of this book?

What words are repeated?

Do any lines stand out? Which ones?

What was confusing?

Convicting?

Encouraging?

What do you hope to learn from this study?

Spend some time praying for that hope.

GREETING/SENDER

> *Jude, a servant of Jesus Christ and brother of James, To those who are called, beloved in God the Father and kept for Jesus Christ: May mercy, peace, and love be multiplied to you.*
>
> **JUDE 1-2**

Once upon a time, people wrote letters. There weren't any phones to text or emails to send. There was no FaceTime® or Facebook®; there were no tweets, or even planes, trains, or automobiles to make for a quick way to relay a message. When one person wanted to communicate to another person, they'd write to them.

Of the twenty-seven books in the New Testament, twenty-one of them are Letters or Epistles. As the early church was being established, the apostles and other disciples of Jesus had some things they needed to communicate—things dealing with faith, the gospel, false teaching, and judgment. At times, churches needed to be encouraged, at other times particular churches needed to be rebuked. But the early leaders of the church were not always close by the particular churches or individuals they wanted to communicate with. So they communicated, by inspiration of the Holy Spirit, through letters. These letters would then be received, read, and prayerfully put into practice.

In Greco-Roman times, most letters followed a particular format or structure. Letters almost always began with a greeting. And the greeting typically had the same elements: Name of sender, description of recipient, and a prayer, blessing, or thanksgiving.

In the following examples of New Testament letter greetings,
   1. Underline the sender.
   2. Put brackets around the recipients.
   3. Circle the blessing or thanksgiving.

> *Paul, called by the will of God to be an apostle of Christ Jesus, and our brother Sosthenes, To the church of God that is in Corinth, to those sanctified in Christ Jesus, called to be saints together with all those who in every place call upon the name of our Lord Jesus Christ, both their Lord and ours: Grace to you and peace from God our Father and the Lord Jesus Christ.*
>
> **1 CORINTHIANS 1:1-3**

Paul, an apostle of Christ Jesus by the will of God,
To the saints who are in Ephesus, and are faithful in Christ Jesus: Grace to
you and peace from God our Father and the Lord Jesus Christ.

EPHESIANS 1:1-2

John to the seven churches that are in Asia: Grace to you and peace from
him who is and who was and who is to come, and from the seven spirits who
are before his throne, and from Jesus Christ the faithful witness, the firstborn
of the dead, and the ruler of kings on earth.

REVELATION 1:4-5

Greco-Roman letters, written by Christians and non-Christians alike, followed this format, showing us that the style of these greetings wasn't a particularly Christian thing but a cultural norm.

Here's the greetings portion of a letter written by a Roman soldier named Apion around two thousand years ago.

His greeting reads:
"*Apion to Epimachos, his respected father, very many greetings.*

Most of all I pray that you are in good health and doing well in every way along with my sister and her daughter and my brother. I give thanks to the Lord Sarapis [an Egyptian god] because, when I was in danger at sea, he saved me straight away."[1]

In Apion's greeting:
   1. Underline the sender.
   2. Put brackets around the recipients.
   3. Circle the blessing or thanksgiving.

Now, though the *style* of the New Testament writers' letters are similar to Apion's, there is a huge difference between them: the content.

Comparing both greetings (those in the New Testament letters versus Apion's), what's the major difference in their content?

In Apion's letter on the right, he includes Sarapis, an Egyptian god which we know to be no god at all, in his greeting. In New Testament greetings, the true and living God is always put on display. New Testament greetings are able to teach us a lot about the personhood of God in just a few sentences.

Let's read one of Paul's densest greetings in Romans 1:1-7. Below, list everything Paul says about God.

Here's everything I learned about God from this greeting:

- God has a gospel.
- God's gospel was promised beforehand through His prophets.
- God's gospel concerns His Son.
- God's Son was descended from David, according to the flesh.
- Christ was declared as the Son of God, according to the Spirit.
- The Spirit is holy.
- Christ resurrected from the dead.
- Jesus Christ is Lord.
- Jesus Christ is gracious.
- Jesus gives apostleship.
- He does it for the sake of His name.
- There are people called to belong to Christ.
- God loves.
- God calls saints.
- God is a Father.
- God the Father and Jesus Christ the Lord have grace and peace to give.

Who would think you could find out so much about God in a simple greeting! This is why we shouldn't skip them in our reading and study of the Bible. "All Scripture is breathed out by God and profitable for teaching, for reproof, for correction, and for training in righteousness" (2 Tim. 3:16). That *all* means every single greeting has something in it that God will use to teach us, reprove us, correct us, and train us in righteousness. These greetings are not arbitrary; they too are God's words to us.

SENDER

Read Jude 1-2.

Who is the sender of the letter and what does the greeting tell us about him?

This word *servant* is *doulos* in the Greek which is translated as "slave" or "servant." The definition of *doulos,* or slave, is "a person who is legally owned by someone else and a person whose entire livelihood and purpose is determined by their master."[2] The word *slave* carries a lot of baggage in our culture. It brings to mind pictures of human beings made in the image of God, being taken captive to do the will of evil men and women. The word is used differently here. Jude was not a slave to men, but God—meaning Jude listened to, followed, obeyed, and honored God. Jude had no intention of living for anything other than the will of God.

Jude followed in the footsteps of others who identified themselves as a *doulos* or slave of God:

Pick three of the following passages to look up. List the names of other people who were either called servants of God by others or called themselves servants of God.

- **Genesis 26:24**

- **Exodus 14:31**

- **Judges 2:8**

- **1 Samuel 1:10-11**

- **2 Samuel 7:20-21**

- **Romans 1:1**

- **2 Peter 1:1**

Jude calling himself "servant" was not only a marker of his humility and sense of purpose, but it would have also been understood by his listeners as a title of honor. Jude was among the likes of men and women God used to do great things. Being a slave of Christ had honor, not because of Jude, but because of who Jude served.

In Jude's greeting, who did he say he was a slave to? List two verses that would help someone get to know him.

Read Matthew 13:53-55 in your Bible. How does Jude know Jesus? (Jude is a nickname for Judas.[3])

Look at how Jude described his relationship to Jesus in Jude 1 and compare it to how Matthew 13:55 describes Jude's relationship with Jesus. What does this tell you about Jude's character?

Which relative of Jesus and Jude is mentioned in both verse 1 of Jude and Matthew 13:55? Look at Galatians 2:9 and record how Paul described this particular relative.

If James was a prominent figure in the early church, how do you think Jude's recipients would have viewed Jude's authority to write this particular Epistle?

Jude's greeting was his introduction to this particular group of Christians to which he has a message for. Before he jumped straight into his message (like the writer of Hebrews), he introduced himself. And because greetings are profitable for us, surely there was *something* we learned about God or even ourselves as we read.

RECIPIENTS

> *To those who are called, beloved in God the Father and kept for Jesus Christ ...*
> **JUDE 1b**

With any letter, knowing the sender gives us some context while we're reading what's been written. Knowing who the recipient is remains just as important; it helps us know who the letter is for. In addition, we can get a grasp on how the sender viewed the people to whom he was speaking and how it shaped what he communicated to them. The way Jude viewed his recipients, according to verse 1, should be understood as how God viewed the recipients.

What three words are used to describe the recipients?

CALLED

What do you think of when you hear the word called?

Look up these passages in your Bible and pay attention to how the word *called* **is used in each passage.**

- *Romans 8:28-30*

- *1 Corinthians 1:4-9*

- *2 Thessalonians 2:13-14*

- *2 Timothy 1:8-9*

In your own words, what can you gather about the word called from these texts?

Those whom God has called have been summoned into fellowship with Jesus Christ (1 Cor. 1:9). God's call is not merely an invitation to know Him, but it is a call that inevitably leads to faith in Him (Rom. 8:30). And this calling deals with our past, present, and future.

Read Jude 24.

Jude most likely knew this was where he was heading in his Letter. What could he have been preparing his recipients to understand about the connection between God's calling and God's keeping?

How might the recipients of Jude's Letter have been encouraged by remembering they'd been called? (Reread Jude to answer this question.)

BELOVED IN GOD THE FATHER

Define the word below. (Look it up if you need help.)

Beloved

_____

_____

_____

_____

The recipients of Jude's Letter had been effectually called by God and were also loved by God. Do you think God's love motivated His call? Explain by using Scripture(s) to defend your position. (For example, Jesus loved and called His disciples in John 1.)

Jude's recipients were called and loved by God.

What do Genesis 1:1, Isaiah 6:1-5, and Isaiah 44:6-8 tell us about God?

How does Romans 3:10-18,23 describe all people?

How does Ephesians 2:1-3 describe all of humankind's behavior toward God? All of humankind is what by nature?

Considering who God the Father is and who the recipients of Jude's Letter were, how should the statement "beloved in God the Father" be received (Jude 1b)?

Circling back to the fact that these people (once unrighteous/children of wrath) have been *called* by God—there is no reason for their being called by God other than the reality that they are loved by God.

Read Ephesians 2:4-10.

What affection preceded God's actions according to this passage?

What did God do for those He had called so they might walk in what He's called them to do?

How might the recipients of Jude's Letter have been encouraged by remembering they were "beloved in God the Father" (Jude 1b)? (Reread Jude to answer this question.)

KEPT FOR JESUS CHRIST

In Day 1, you were asked if you saw any words being repeated in Jude's Letter. How many times did you see the words kept *or* keep*?*

God's protection of those He's called and those He loves seems to be an important idea that Jude wants to communicate. His repetition of the word *kept* or *keep* seems to highlight this emphasis.

To be kept by or for Jesus Christ (depending on your Bible translation) isn't unique to Jude. Let's read about the time Jesus spoke to the Father about the same thing. Underline each use of the word kept *or* keep*.*

And I am no longer in the world, but they are in the world, and I am coming to you. Holy Father, keep them in your name, which you have given me, that they may be one, even as we are one. While I was with them, I kept them in your name, which you have given me. I have guarded them, and not one of them has been lost except the son of destruction, that the Scripture might be fulfilled. But now I am coming to you, and these things I speak in the world, that they may have my joy fulfilled in themselves. I have given them your word, and the world has hated them because they are not of the world, just as I am not of the world. I do not ask that you take them out of the world, but that you keep them from the evil one.

JOHN 17:11-15

Before Jesus was to leave earth, one of the concerns, and thus petitions, of His heart was for God to protect, guard, and keep the ones that had been given to Him. Jesus was aware of the temptations of the evil one and the lures of the world. He knew if God's hand did not hold His own, His own would fall.

So Jesus prayed for His own to be kept.

And Jude, Jesus' brother and servant, says they are.

To Keep: to maintain; to be kept in a certain state, position, or activity.[4]

Let's look at some other times this word *kept* is used in Scripture to see if we can get a sense of its meaning.

So Peter was kept in prison, but earnest prayer for him was made to God by the church.

ACTS 12:5

Festus replied that Paul was being kept at Caesarea and that he himself intended to go there shortly.

ACTS 25:4

Read the verses below and answer the questions that follow:

> *Blessed be the God and Father of our Lord Jesus Christ! According to his great mercy, he has caused us to be born again to a living hope through the resurrection of Jesus Christ from the dead, to an inheritance that is imperishable, undefiled, and unfading, kept in heaven for you.*
> **1 PETER 1:3-4**

Those who have been born again have an inheritance in heaven that is being _____.

• **Is it secure?**

• **Is it safe?**

• **Can it be moved?**

• **Can it be taken?**

• **Why?**

Just as Peter was kept in prison, Paul was kept in Caesarea, and your inheritance is being kept in heaven. Jude told the people he was writing to that they too were being kept for Jesus Christ.

This letter is about to get pretty intense and challenging to its readers. But before then, Jude makes sure to remind his recipients of God's call to them, God's love for them, and God's protection of them. We can learn a lot from Jude on what it looks like to encourage the ones you are about to challenge, especially in terms of identity. Jude affirmed their identities in a very God-centric way (called *by* God, loved *in* God, kept *for* God). He didn't neglect God to build them up, nor did he neglect them. He glorified God and loved them well.

BLESSING

> *May mercy, peace, and love be multiplied to you.*
> **JUDE 2**

The concept of blessing reaches all the way back to Genesis (Gen. 1:28). Blessings, or benedictions as they are also called, were pronounced by Old Testament kings (for example, Gen. 14:18-20 and 2 Sam. 6:20), family members (for example, Gen. 49:1-28 and Ruth 1:8-9), and priests—the group we're about to look at. Simply put, these blessings were prayers directed toward God but said aloud to the people the blessings were intended for. And though the benedictions in Scripture may seem trite, they are far from it. They carry a lot of weight when considered in light of who we ask the blessings for and who the blessings come from.

Turn in your Bible to Numbers 6:22-27.

Who speaks the blessing?

Who does the blessing?

What are the blessings?

Notice, Aaron asks for the Lord to keep Israel. And in Day 3, we saw that God's covenant people (the new Israel) *are* being kept.

Turn to Ruth 1:8-9.

Who speaks the blessing?

Who does the blessing?

What are the blessings?

In both blessings, we see three consistent ideas. The people of God pray for blessings for other people of God. All of the requested blessings have one source, God. And all of these blessings seek the welfare of the recipient.

That pattern continues in the New Testament.

Turn to Hebrews 13:20-21.

Who speaks the blessing?

Who does the blessing?

What are the blessings?

In the New Testament Epistles, it is common for the blessing to be present in the greeting, one of the most popular blessings being Paul's use of "Grace to you and peace from God our Father and the Lord Jesus Christ" (1 Cor. 1:3; 2 Cor. 1:2; Gal. 1:3; Eph 1:2; Phil. 1:2).

If you think about it, how encouraging would it be to receive a prayer of blessing upon being greeted?

Jude didn't neglect this practice. Before he got to the nitty-gritty of his letter, he ended his greeting with a prayer of blessing for his recipients.

Look at Jude 2.

Who speaks the blessing?

Who does the blessing?

What are the blessings?

Let's dig into the biblical definitions of these words of blessing and look at them in the context of Jude's Letter.

MERCY

Define:

Mercy _____

_____

_____

_____

Remember what we learned about God and Jude's recipients in Day 3? What kind of people were they? And how did their description contrast with who God is?

Read Jude 14-15 along with Ephesians 2:1-9. If God wasn't merciful toward Jude's recipients (and us), what would they have received from God?

According to Romans 9:14-18, God has mercy on whom?

In your own words, describe God's mercy.

Read over Jude. Why would Jude's recipients have needed a prayer for mercy? Use specific examples from the text to explain.

PEACE

Define:

Peace

_____

_____

_____

_____

There are two ways to understand peace. There is peace *with* God and peace *from* God.

PEACE *WITH* GOD

According to James 4:4, what's the relationship between God and friends of the world?

Circle the word in the passage below that speaks to the opposite of being at peace with God:

> *For the mind that is set on the flesh is hostile to God, for it does not submit to God's law; indeed, it cannot. Those who are in the flesh cannot please God.*
> **ROMANS 8:7-8**

The words "hostile" and "enemy" both give the image of the real tension that existed between us and God.

Read Romans 5:1.

How does it say we have received peace with God?

PEACE *FROM* GOD

Having peace *with* God opened up the door for us to have peace *from* God. Jude was not praying for the Christians who would read his letter to be at peace *with* God—they already were at peace with God. Jude was praying for them to be blessed with peace *from* God.

> *Peace I leave with you; my peace I give to you. Not as the world gives do I give to you. Let not your hearts be troubled, neither let them be afraid.*
> **JOHN 14:27**

A blessed change takes place in the sinner's state, when he becomes a true believer, whatever he has been. Being justified by faith he has peace with God. The holy, righteous God, cannot be at peace with a sinner, while under the guilt of sin. Justification takes away the guilt, and so makes way for peace.[5]

MATTHEW HENRY

What does the peace that Jesus gives (not worldly peace) do for the heart?

Read over Jude again. Why would Jude's recipients have needed his prayer for peace? Use specific examples from the text to explain. (For example: verse 4 might have induced paranoia, verse 22 might have lead to frustration.)

At the individual level, this peace secures composure in the midst of trouble, and dissolves fear, as the final injunction of this verse demonstrates. This is the peace which garrisons our hearts and minds against the invasion of anxiety (Phil. 4:7), and rules or arbitrates in the hearts of God's people to maintain harmony amongst them (Col. 3:15).[6]

D. A. CARSON

LOVE

Define:

Love

_____

_____

_____

_____

Read Romans 5:6-9.

How do all four of these verses explain God's love?

Read 1 John 3:1-2.

How do these verses explain God's love? Be specific but don't just copy and paste. Actually sit with the passage, thinking through the way it describes God's love.

Why would Jude's recipients have needed a prayer for love? Use specific examples from the text to explain. (Pay special attention to the instructions Jude provides.)

Jude asked for God's mercy, peace, and love to be multiplied to them, or in other words, for mercy, peace, and love to continually overflow toward the recipients of the letter. What would it have looked like for Jude's recipients to overflow in mercy, peace, and love?

JUDE 3-4

As you watch the Week 2 video, answer the following questions:

- What did Jude originally plan to write about? What did he write instead?
- What must we contend for? Who is Jude telling to contend?
- What is at stake when we deny God?

After watching the Week 2 video, discuss the following together as a group:

- Who were you before God came into your life? Describe the change that occurred in you.
- Is there an incorrect way to contend for the faith?
- Have you ever heard a friend making false claims about Jesus or Christianity? Did you correct his or her wrong assumptions? Why or why not?
- How can you recognize false teachers?
- How can we proclaim to know God, but still deny Him through our works?

_____

_____

_____

_____

_____

_____

_____

_____

_____

_____

> BELOVED, ALTHOUGH I WAS VERY EAGER TO WRITE TO YOU ABOUT OUR COMMON SALVATION, I FOUND IT NECESSARY TO WRITE APPEALING TO YOU TO CONTEND FOR THE FAITH THAT WAS ONCE FOR ALL DELIVERED TO THE SAINTS. ⁴FOR CERTAIN PEOPLE HAVE CREPT IN UNNOTICED WHO LONG AGO WERE DESIGNATED FOR THIS CONDEMNATION, UNGODLY PEOPLE, WHO PERVERT THE GRACE OF OUR GOD INTO SENSUALITY AND DENY OUR ONLY MASTER AND LORD, JESUS CHRIST.
>
> JUDE 3-4

Every letter has a reason for being written. When couples write each other, we expect the content to be lovely—affectionate words thrown into sentences so the recipient can feel the love that is being expressed from a distance. At some point, maybe in the beginning or toward the end, the writer will include his or her "why." It might be "I wrote this because I love you." Or "I wrote this because I wanted you to remember what we share." Either way, the recipient understands the whole reason for why the letter was written and is then able to move forward in how he or she should respond. If insecurities might have existed, remembering the recipient's love that they've been tempted to question creates a calm in the distant recipient.

In Jude's letter, there is an aim behind his words. He has written a letter full of grace and truth for a reason, and this reason demands a response.

COMMON SALVATION

> *Beloved, although I was very eager to write to you about our common salvation, I found it necessary to write appealing to you to contend for the faith that was once for all delivered to the saints.*
> **JUDE 3**

What did Jude intend to write about?

In your own words, what is salvation?

Why do we all need salvation anyway? (Remember what we learned in the Week 2 video about mercy to help formulate your answer.)

Carefully read over Jude and mark every occurrence of the word *saved*.

Considering the way *saved* is used in these verses, what do you think Jude intended?

In the following verses, pay attention to what the recipients were saved from. Record your observations after each passage.

> *Now I want to remind you, although you once fully knew it, that Jesus, who saved a people out of the land of Egypt, afterward destroyed those who did not believe.*
>
> **JUDE 5**

> *... save others by snatching them out of the fire; to others show mercy with fear, hating even the garment stained by the flesh.*
>
> **JUDE 23**

> *Now to him who is able to keep you from stumbling and to present you blameless before the presence of his glory with great joy, to the only God, our Savior, through Jesus Christ our Lord, be glory, majesty, dominion, and authority, before all time and now and forever. Amen.*
>
> **JUDE 24-25**

Salvation is a great biblical word, but too often it is allowed to slip from its biblical moorings. We often use the idea of "being saved" as if it were identical to "being converted" or "being a Christian." But it is much richer than that. Jude's most famous verses (24-25) praise "God our Saviour," and it is clear from the context there that he means that God will save us in the future.[1]

DICK LUCAS AND CHRISTOPHER GREEN

Those who have been *saved* have been saved *from* something. Salvation is the act of being rescued from danger (destruction, fire, stumbling) and being delivered into a place of safety (out of Egypt, out of fire, presented blameless).

From what we've learned about salvation so far, how does salvation have an impact on our future reality?

Read the following verses and note the past, present, and future tense that corresponds with each verse.

For by grace you have been saved through faith. And this is not your own doing; it is the gift of God.

EPHESIANS 2:8

***Salvation is a reality of the** _____.*

For the word of the cross is folly to those who are perishing, but to us who are being saved it is the power of God.

1 CORINTHIANS 1:18

***Salvation is a reality in the** _____.*

Since, therefore, we have now been justified by his blood, much more shall we be saved by him from the wrath of God.

ROMANS 5:9

***Salvation is a reality of the** _____.*

Salvation was secured when Jesus died and rose for those whom God has called, but it didn't stop at our being rescued from the power of sin (regeneration) and the guilt of sin (justification). It is a complete work in that our salvation will culminate in our being saved from the wrath of God that is to come.

Keep this in mind as we go throughout our study because as we noted earlier, the idea of salvation occurs over and over throughout Jude's letter. As we journey through this book, we will discover why the future salvation of the beloved of God and the called of God is an important reality for them to hold onto.

Read over Jude and list three reasons why you think salvation is a theme throughout Jude's Epistle. As we study more, you will be able to see if your initial thoughts were correct.

1. _____

2. _____

3. _____

EAGER VS. NECESSARY

Before Jude sat down to put pen to paper (or ink to parchment), he had every intention of writing about the salvation they all shared. But at hearing there were people among the recipients who were denying Christ Jesus and perverting His grace into sensuality, he was compelled to write another letter.

Has there ever been a time when you wanted to minister to someone about something that was good and true, but ended up choosing the route of what was necessary for them to hear instead? If yes, explain.

What compelled you to say the necessary thing?

Have you ever had a time when you knew what needed to be said but you decided not to? If yes, explain.

What compelled you not to say the necessary thing?

Define:

Eager

_____

_____

_____

_____

COMMON SALVATION: Salvation isn't reserved for a particular kind of person. Important people don't get first dibs on salvation. People who might think themselves to be more moral than others don't either. God's offer of salvation is given to all. John 3:16 says that "whoever" believes in Christ shall not perish but have eternal life, meaning anybody, anywhere. No matter the age, socioeconomic status, ethnicity, or even sin preference, salvation can happen for and to them. This salvation is common because it is shared by many and is available to anyone who chooses to believe in Christ Jesus.

Circle the synonyms for eager:

Intent	Unenthusiastic	Dispassionate	Unconcerned
Earnest	Ready	Willing	Disinterested
Apathetic	Effort	Longing	

Define:

Necessary _____

_____

_____

_____

Circle the synonyms for necessary:

Trivial	Mandatory	Optional	Inessential
Imperative	Urgent	Needed	Paramount
Unimportant	Vital	Unavoidable	

Which of the synonyms you circled line up with why you were compelled to say the necessary thing?

Which of the antonyms you skipped line up with what compelled you not to say the necessary thing?

Just like Jude, we all, at some point, will find ourselves needing to discern between what we really want to say to someone and what we need to say. If we're honest, our fears and lack of love can mix with what we're willing to discuss. When that happens, we might be willing to tell the truth, but we also might stick to those truths that aren't as difficult to share. Jude's prayer for his recipients to abound in love was being modeled by Jude in how eager he was to tell his readers what they needed to hear.

Read Jude 3-4.

What's going on in his readers' lives that compelled Jude to write this letter?

How do you usually discern what's necessary to say?

Jude had been made aware of people among God's beloved who were dangerous to the recipients' faith and commitment to their Savior. Jude discerns what was necessary for him to say by his knowledge of their context. Therefore, he knew what he should say because he knew what was actually going on in their lives. Not only that, Jude knew what could happen if they were not warned. He had wisdom that had been shaped by the Scriptures, wisdom that not only helped him to discern what was necessary but also why it was necessary.

In Paul's letter to the Galatians, we find another example of the importance of being aware of context and having the wisdom needed to warn.

Turn to Galatians 1:6-9 in your Bible.
   What is going on in their context?

Why does Paul warn them? (Fill in the blanks.)
- **Galatians 3:10:** Because they will be _____ for relying on works of the law.
- **Galatians 5:1:** Because they will _____ to a yoke of slavery.
- **Galatians 5:4:** Because they will be _____ from Christ.
- **Galatians 5:4:** Because they will _____ _____ from grace.
- **Galatians 5:7:** Because they will be _____ from obeying the truth.

Paul did what was necessary by writing the Galatians and warning them of what would happen if they chose to trust in a false gospel, and Jude was doing the same. There were people in their midst whose end was sure, and Jude wanted to make sure his recipients didn't find themselves following in their footsteps oblivious to where they would lead. He urgently wanted for them to contend for the faith that was being threatened.

What are some of the pressing issues going on in your life that would be necessary for you to address?

The world: **Your neighborhood:**

Your country: **Your home:**

Your city: **Your church:**

Ask God for the wisdom and the boldness and the love to address each whenever you are given the opportunity.

DAY 2

CONTENDING BY FAITH

> *I found it necessary to write appealing to you to contend for the faith that was once for all delivered to the saints.*
>
> **JUDE 3b**

> *You stand up to his side, attack with your foot and fight it out.*
> *You throw him. You stand up and turn around. You fight it out.*
> *You throw him. You sweep and knock his foot out.*
> *Stand to the side of your opponent and with your right arm take a headlock and fight it out.*
> *You take a hold around him. You get under his hold. You step through and fight it out.*
> *You underhook with your right arm. You wrap your arm around his, where he has taken the underhook, and attack the side with your left foot. You push away with your left hand. You force the hold and fight it out.*
> *You turn around. You fight it out with a grip on both sides.*
> *You throw your foot forward. You take a hold around his body. You step forward and force his head back. You face him and bend back and throw yourself into him, bracing your foot.[2]*
> **A literal English translation of the *Papyrus Oxyrhynchus III, 466***

What you've just read are second-century wrestling instructions, originally written in Greek, and most likely intended for a man training for the Olympic games. Among other sports such as boxing, chariot racing, and the long jump, wrestling was a popular sport among Greeks. One reason being that wrestling was innately connected to warfare.[3] Two men engaged in a struggle until one came out the victor was entertaining as well as inspiring.

This image of one person fighting, resisting, grabbing, bracing, attacking, out of breath yet focused, with as much perseverance as is needed to finish what's been started, is the image Jude was evoking when he told his recipients that he wanted them to "contend for the faith."

Contend: in Greek *agónízomai*, from the root of the English term, "agonize" meaning "properly, to struggle, like engaged in an intense athletic contest or warfare"[4]

Later in Jude's letter, he would give instructions on how to contend for the faith. But for now, let's learn from him and other passages of Scripture on how *not* to contend.

Describe a time when you've seen someone else contend or when you have personally contended for the faith in a manner that misrepresented the faith:

Circle some of the characteristics that were present:

Gentle	*Irritable*	*Quick to listen*	*Judgmental*
Angry	*Kindness*	*Tense*	*Personable*
Calm	*Mocking*	*Welcoming*	*Distant*
Slow to Speak	*Interrupting*	*Empathetic*	*Arrogant*

Contending for the faith has led many to defend the faith with great zeal and minimal love. We've seen it on the news and all over our social media. Many of us, before coming to faith, probably had our own encounters with people who wanted to introduce us to Jesus and all that He taught, but they actually failed to display Jesus in how they taught.

How we, as God's beloved, contend for the faith matters.

In your own Bible, read 1 Peter 3:15.

What are the two characteristics Peter says we should display when making a defense?
   1.

   2.

Now read 2 Timothy 2:24-26.

What shouldn't the Lord's servant (same word Jude uses to describe himself in verse 1) be?

What should the Lord's servant be?
   1.

   2.

   3.

   4.

Read Colossians 4:5-6.

How should we walk with outsiders?

How should we speak?

Do you think that these exhortations are easy to obey? Why or why not?

The exhortations in these verses seem simple enough. Be kind? That's easy! Be gentle? No problem! But clearly, if they were easy to do, we'd see those verses obeyed more often.

Let's read a verse that might give us a clue as to why contending for the faith has been mishandled so badly, so often.

> *Now the works of the flesh are evident: sexual immorality, impurity, sensuality, idolatry, sorcery, enmity, strife, jealousy, fits of anger, rivalries, dissensions, divisions, envy, drunkenness, orgies, and things like these. I warn you, as I warned you before, that those who do such things will not inherit the kingdom of God. But the fruit of the Spirit is love, joy, peace, patience, kindness, goodness, faithfulness, gentleness, self-control; against such things there is no law. And those who belong to Christ Jesus have crucified the flesh with its passions and desires.*
> **GALATIANS 5:19-24**

The works of the flesh are a long list of behaviors/attitudes that come about when someone is not walking according to the Spirit. Did you notice any words listed that fit with the behaviors of someone contending for the faith in the wrong way?

List them:

The fruit of the Spirit are behaviors/attitudes that come about when someone is being led by the Spirit. Did you notice any behaviors listed that fit with the behaviors that someone contending for the faith in the right way would display?

List them:

How we contend for the faith will have everything to do with whether we are being led by the Spirit when we do it. The kindness, gentleness, patience, and wisdom God is calling us to display will only be present in us when we let the Spirit guide us. It is natural for us to argue when attacked or to speak more than we listen. We are all prone toward being easily irritated when someone "just doesn't get it." Or to resort to harsh words when we've grown tired (impatience) of being kind. But those who belong to Christ Jesus have crucified the flesh (Gal. 5:24) and are more than able to walk by the Spirit. That is good news! We don't have to be named among those who contend for the faith in an ungodly manner, but we can be young women who fight for the faith by the Spirit.

Look at the Greek definition of contend again. What English word stems from it?

To agonize over something is to "struggle" over it.[5] A struggle can take time, a lot of energy, and thought. A struggle can be quick, but it can also be something that takes a bit of time and thus perseverance.

Thinking through what it would look like to struggle with others in defense of God's Word and the explicit teachings in Scripture that our culture fights so hard to defy, what does Jude's use of the word agónízomai (contend) do for your understanding of how you should approach contending for the faith?

Contending for the faith is not the same as being contentious for the faith or even being critical in the name of the faith. That's not God's character or Jude's heart here. He's simply urging the church to defend the truth. By doing so, God's church will actually be the church. We want people to look at us and see Jesus, and to see Jesus they must understand the truth.

THE FAITH

> *I found it necessary to write appealing to you to contend for the faith that was once for all delivered to the saints.*
>
> **JUDE 3b**

So now we know that we, as Christians, are supposed to contend. And our contending should be done by the Spirit, so that in our contending, Jesus shines. The next question is: *What are we actually contending for?* In the Ancient Greco-Roman times, during the Olympic Games, men were contending for an olive wreath. It was their objective goal. Wrestle for the wreath. Fight for the wreath. Struggle for the wreath.

Jude tells his recipients in verse 3: the objective goal they are to wrestle for, fight for, and struggle for is the faith.

Now, it might be natural for us to read the word *faith* and think it's referring to faith as in the belief or confidence we've placed in the person and Word of God through Jesus Christ. But let's compare some texts that include the same word to identify what Jude meant by it.

> **Compare the implied meaning of the word faith in Hebrews 11:1 and 2 Corinthians 5:7 to how it's used in Galatians 1:23 and Acts 6:7.**

> **Which group do you think would best apply to what Jude means by the faith? (Feel free to use the cross-references provided in your Bible.) How does it provide clarity to what the faith is?**

> **If the faith refers to "the body of Christian doctrine"[7] and Jude was saying we must contend and defend it, would it be safe to say that contending for the faith must include actually communicating about the faith? Why or why not?**

CROSS-REFERENCE: to reference another part of the text. Many Bibles have verses in the margin, marked by a superscript letter to help you cross reference one passage to another.

Underline the references made to teaching in the passages below:

> And Jesus came and said to them, "All authority in heaven and on earth has been given to me. Go therefore and make disciples of all nations, baptizing them in the name of the Father and of the Son and of the Holy Spirit, teaching them to observe all that I have commanded you."
> **MATTHEW 28:18-20a**

> And the Lord's servant must not be quarrelsome but kind to everyone, able to teach, patiently enduring evil, correcting his opponents with gentleness. God may perhaps grant them repentance leading to a knowledge of the truth, and they may come to their senses and escape from the snare of the devil, after being captured by him to do his will.
>
> **2 TIMOTHY 2:24-26**

> "The faith" refers to Christian doctrine, the apostles' teaching, Jesus' teaching given to the apostles, the divinely inspired doctrine given by God to the apostles. He wants them to cling to that faith and to contend for that faith, the apostles' teaching, the body of Christian doctrine.[6]
>
> **LIGON DUNCAN**

Paul says the Lord's servant must be able to teach (ready/capable of teaching) and that they must correct opponents (point out error and redirect to the truth).

Explain why being able to teach and correcting opponents are important in contending for the faith.

In Jesus' commission of His disciples, He told them to teach all that He'd commanded. When making a defense for the faith, how does our own knowledge of the Word of God help us in teaching it to others?

You can't teach what you don't know. You can't correct what you never learned.

We equip ourselves to contend for the faith by the study of God's Word. Though it is helpful to be aware of many of the lies being preached, tweeted, quoted, and lived as it will help us in our preparation of making a defense (1 Pet. 3:15), we don't necessarily need to know every single false teaching or misrepresentation of Scripture to be able to address it. By knowing the Word of God, you'll be able to discern error in the message or life of another (Heb. 5:14), so you can gently guide them toward the truth.

Now what is *the faith*, as in, what are the essential doctrines of Scripture Christians must contend for?

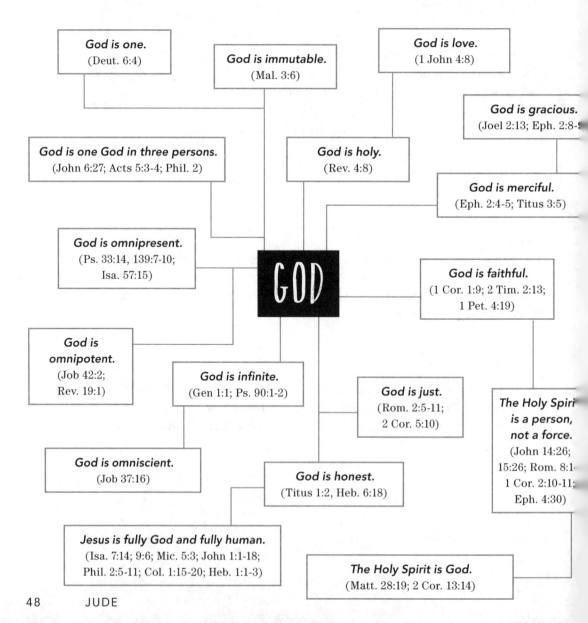

God is one.
(Deut. 6:4)

God is immutable.
(Mal. 3:6)

God is love.
(1 John 4:8)

God is gracious.
(Joel 2:13; Eph. 2:8-9)

God is one God in three persons.
(John 6:27; Acts 5:3-4; Phil. 2)

God is holy.
(Rev. 4:8)

God is merciful.
(Eph. 2:4-5; Titus 3:5)

God is omnipresent.
(Ps. 33:14, 139:7-10; Isa. 57:15)

GOD

God is faithful.
(1 Cor. 1:9; 2 Tim. 2:13; 1 Pet. 4:19)

God is omnipotent.
(Job 42:2; Rev. 19:1)

God is infinite.
(Gen 1:1; Ps. 90:1-2)

God is just.
(Rom. 2:5-11; 2 Cor. 5:10)

The Holy Spirit is a person, not a force.
(John 14:26; 15:26; Rom. 8:14; 1 Cor. 2:10-11; Eph. 4:30)

God is omniscient.
(Job 37:16)

God is honest.
(Titus 1:2, Heb. 6:18)

Jesus is fully God and fully human.
(Isa. 7:14; 9:6; Mic. 5:3; John 1:1-18; Phil. 2:5-11; Col. 1:15-20; Heb. 1:1-3)

The Holy Spirit is God.
(Matt. 28:19; 2 Cor. 13:14)

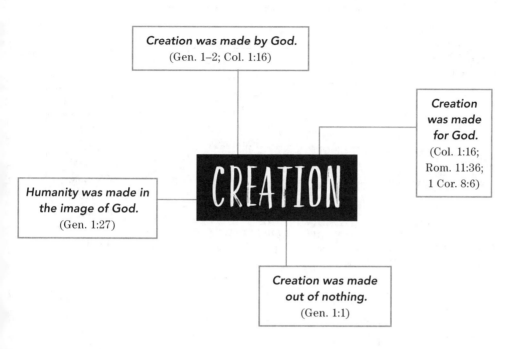

Creation was made by God.
(Gen. 1–2; Col. 1:16)

Creation was made for God.
(Col. 1:16; Rom. 11:36; 1 Cor. 8:6)

Humanity was made in the image of God.
(Gen. 1:27)

CREATION

Creation was made out of nothing.
(Gen. 1:1)

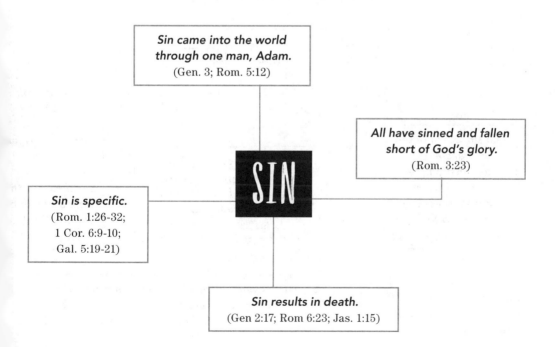

Sin came into the world through one man, Adam.
(Gen. 3; Rom. 5:12)

All have sinned and fallen short of God's glory.
(Rom. 3:23)

Sin is specific.
(Rom. 1:26-32; 1 Cor. 6:9-10; Gal. 5:19-21)

SIN

Sin results in death.
(Gen 2:17; Rom 6:23; Jas. 1:15)

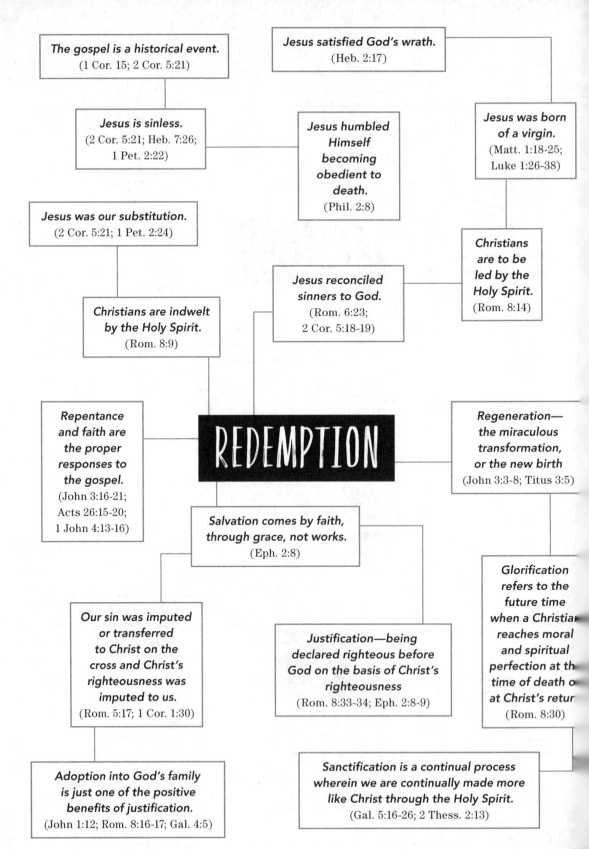

The gospel is a historical event.
(1 Cor. 15; 2 Cor. 5:21)

Jesus satisfied God's wrath.
(Heb. 2:17)

Jesus is sinless.
(2 Cor. 5:21; Heb. 7:26;
1 Pet. 2:22)

Jesus humbled Himself becoming obedient to death.
(Phil. 2:8)

Jesus was born of a virgin.
(Matt. 1:18-25;
Luke 1:26-38)

Jesus was our substitution.
(2 Cor. 5:21; 1 Pet. 2:24)

Jesus reconciled sinners to God.
(Rom. 6:23;
2 Cor. 5:18-19)

Christians are to be led by the Holy Spirit.
(Rom. 8:14)

Christians are indwelt by the Holy Spirit.
(Rom. 8:9)

Repentance and faith are the proper responses to the gospel.
(John 3:16-21;
Acts 26:15-20;
1 John 4:13-16)

REDEMPTION

Regeneration—the miraculous transformation, or the new birth
(John 3:3-8; Titus 3:5)

Salvation comes by faith, through grace, not works.
(Eph. 2:8)

Our sin was imputed or transferred to Christ on the cross and Christ's righteousness was imputed to us.
(Rom. 5:17; 1 Cor. 1:30)

Justification—being declared righteous before God on the basis of Christ's righteousness
(Rom. 8:33-34; Eph. 2:8-9)

Glorification refers to the future time when a Christian reaches moral and spiritual perfection at the time of death or at Christ's return
(Rom. 8:30)

Adoption into God's family is just one of the positive benefits of justification.
(John 1:12; Rom. 8:16-17; Gal. 4:5)

Sanctification is a continual process wherein we are continually made more like Christ through the Holy Spirit.
(Gal. 5:16-26; 2 Thess. 2:13)

Adapted from "The 99 Essential Doc
The Gospel Projec

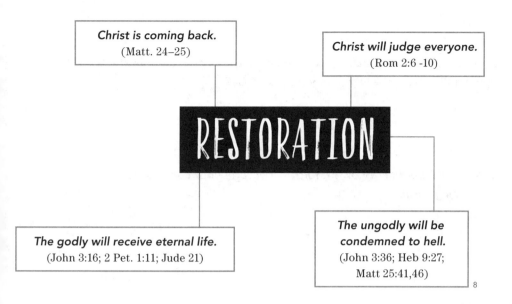

Which of the five essentials of the faith (God, creation, sin, redemption, restoration) do you feel well-equipped to contend for?

Which of the five essentials of the faith do you feel ill-equipped to contend for?

In your own cultural context, what essentials of the faith do you find yourself having to address consistently?

At the end of verse 3, Jude says that the faith was delivered to the saints "once for all."

What do you think this phrase means?

If someone were to teach a new revelation that's not found in the Bible, how would verse 3 help you in your response?

How should the finality of the faith encourage your confidence in contending for it?

DAY 4

UNNOTICED TEACHERS

> For certain people have crept in unnoticed who long ago were designated for this condemnation, ungodly people, who pervert the grace of our God into sensuality and deny our only Master and Lord, Jesus Christ.
>
> **JUDE 4**

Look up these verses in your Bible:
- *Matthew 7:15*
- *Acts 20:29-30*
- *2 Peter 2:1*

In what you've just read, what do the false teachers described in each passage have in common?

Jude said the false teachers among his recipients had crept in unnoticed. What do you suppose that means?

"Crept in unnoticed" is from the Greek *pareisdy(n)ō*, which means "to settle in alongside, i.e. lodge stealthily:—creep in unawares."[9]

Clearly, the secret nature by which false teachers invade Christian churches is common. Jesus told us that would be the case. We see it in the teachings of Paul as well. And in Jude's Epistle, among others, it's confirmed; false teachers have come and will stay as long as they can. It's their going "unnoticed" that allows them to continue leading and wooing Christians away from the faith that was delivered to them.

Why do you think false teaching and teachers are able to go unnoticed?

What should we do to ensure that when false teachers are among us, we will notice them?

Let's revisit a verse, but this time read a few of the sentences after it too.

Read Matthew 7:15-20.

How do you recognize false teachers?

In Jude 4, what word describes the character of the false teachers among them?

Read over Jude and count how many times *ungodly* **is used. Write down the number of times it appears:**

Define:

Ungodly _____

_____

_____

_____

What does ungodliness actually look like?

In Galatians 5:19-21, Paul described behaviors considered to be "works of the flesh." What are they?

Those who walk by flesh and not the Spirit are considered to be ungodly. Identifying ungodliness will help us to identify the ungodly. And by identifying the ungodly, we will not be caught off guard by them if and when they begin to teach doctrines that aren't in accordance with godliness (1 Tim. 6:3).

What did Jude say these unnoticed teachers were doing?

God's grace has been misunderstood for centuries, especially among the early church (Rom. 1). Ungodly people among Jude's recipients who have rejected God's grace are now attempting to change the meaning and implications of God's grace.

What do you think it is about grace that causes people to misunderstand it?

What might it look like for someone to "pervert the grace of our God into sensuality" (v. 4)?

If Jude's recipients are to contend for the faith, then they are to contend for the truth of God's grace (an essential aspect of the gospel, the gospel being a part of the faith) and how God's grace should affect the lives of those who've received it. Without a proper understanding of the grace of God, we, along with Jude's recipients, would be susceptible to the teachings of those who would seek to pervert it.

GOD'S GRACE SAVES

Read Ephesians 2:1-10.

List every word that could have described you before you were saved:

1.

2.

3.

4.

5.

6.

List every attribute of God in these verses:

1.

2.

3.

4.

How does comparing Paul's description of us in verses 1-3 and his description of God in verses 4-7 help you to understand verse 8?

In your own words, how would you use Ephesians 2:1-10 to teach about God's grace?

GOD'S GRACE TEACHES

For the grace of God has appeared, bringing salvation for all people, training us to renounce ungodliness and worldly passions, and to live self-controlled, upright, and godly lives in the present age.

TITUS 2:11-12

What does the grace of God train us to renounce (deny or refuse)?

1.

2.

In your own words, how would you use Titus 2:11-12 to teach about God's grace?

Paul's words about God's grace were available to the church(es) that Jude was writing to. They were well acquainted with them. But, the "certain persons" among them were disregarding these clear teachings set in place by the apostles.

What element of God's grace had to be neglected for it to be perverted?

Look up Romans 13:13, Galatians 5:19, and 1 Peter 4:3. Considering the context in which the word sensuality sits in these verses, what might it mean?

Define:

Sensuality _____

_____

_____

_____

With what you know about God's grace and sensuality, in your own words, describe what is happening in verse 4:

Have you ever had someone tell you, or have you ever told yourself, that you can indulge in one or more sins freely because of grace? Describe the situation.

If appealing to God's grace isn't presented as a license to sin, it's common in our culture for people to use God's love as an excuse instead. It's a stance born out of deception and the suppression of truth (Rom. 1:18) because one has to deny the truth of who God is and what He requires to make those kinds of claims. A biblical foundation for understanding the attributes of God equips us against believing this kind of false teaching, and it assists us in challenging those who would dare teach it.

Jude says that these people were perverting grace and denying our only Master and Lord Jesus Christ.

What does it look like to deny Christ?

In your response, if you wrote and therefore thought that denying Christ was a verbal action, you're not wrong in saying so. Denying Christ can be verbal, such as when Peter denied Jesus three times prior to Jesus' crucifixion. Peter's denial of Christ was in the form of words that told his hearers what he wanted them to think about his relationship with Jesus.

But that is not the only way to deny Christ.

Turn in your Bible to Titus 1:16.

How did Titus say these people deny Christ?

Read through Jude. List at least four behaviors that would be a practical denial of Jesus. I'll do the first one for you.

   1. *Indulging in sexual immorality (v. 7)*

   2.

   3.

   4.

Jesus is Master and Lord. To deny His lordship is to live in opposition to reality. Look over the four behaviors you listed on page 58, and consider how different these behavior would look if the people who did them chose to submit to Christ as Master and Lord. I'll do the first one for you.

1. *Instead of indulging in sexual immorality, they would flee sexual immorality and glorify God with their bodies (1 Cor. 6:18-20).*

2.

3.

4.

WEEK 3
JUDE 5-11

As you watch the Week 3 video, answer the following questions:

- Why did the people choose not to enter the Land of Canaan? What was the result of their decision?
- List the two sins that rule over Cain.
- What can we conclude about these unnoticed teachers in Jude?
- What are these people refusing to submit to?
- How are these false teachers disguised?

After watching the Week 3 video, discuss the following together as a group:

- Why would Jude include Old Testament stories as examples in his letter?
- What could false teachers gain by preaching false messages?
- How can you identify false teachers?

NOW I WANT TO REMIND YOU, ALTHOUGH YOU ONCE FULLY KNEW IT, THAT JESUS, WHO SAVED A PEOPLE OUT OF THE LAND OF EGYPT, AFTERWARD DESTROYED THOSE WHO DID NOT BELIEVE. 6AND THE ANGELS WHO DID NOT STAY WITHIN THEIR OWN POSITION OF AUTHORITY, BUT LEFT THEIR PROPER DWELLING, HE HAS KEPT IN ETERNAL CHAINS UNDER GLOOMY DARKNESS UNTIL THE JUDGMENT OF THE GREAT DAY— 7JUST AS SODOM AND GOMORRAH AND THE SURROUNDING CITIES, WHICH LIKEWISE INDULGED IN SEXUAL IMMORALITY AND PURSUED UNNATURAL DESIRE, SERVE AS AN EXAMPLE BY UNDERGOING A PUNISHMENT OF ETERNAL FIRE.

8YET IN LIKE MANNER THESE PEOPLE ALSO, RELYING ON THEIR DREAMS, DEFILE THE FLESH, REJECT AUTHORITY, AND BLASPHEME THE GLORIOUS ONES. 9 BUT WHEN THE ARCHANGEL MICHAEL, CONTENDING WITH THE DEVIL, WAS DISPUTING ABOUT THE BODY OF MOSES, HE DID NOT PRESUME TO PRONOUNCE A BLASPHEMOUS JUDGMENT, BUT SAID, "THE LORD REBUKE YOU. 10BUT THESE PEOPLE BLASPHEME ALL THAT THEY DO NOT UNDERSTAND, AND THEY ARE DESTROYED BY ALL THAT THEY, LIKE UNREASONING ANIMALS, UNDERSTAND INSTINCTIVELY. 11WOE TO THEM! FOR THEY WALKED IN THE WAY OF CAIN AND ABANDONED THEMSELVES FOR THE SAKE OF GAIN TO BALAAM'S ERROR AND PERISHED IN KORAH'S REBELLION.

JUDE 5-11

In the body of Jude's Letter, he connected Old Testament narratives to his New Testament context which provides current day application for us. "These people," as Jude would consistently call them, were teaching that God's grace gives them and others the license to sin, and yet, with such overtly sinful teaching and rebellious lives, these people were going unnoticed. So as a prophetic warning to these men of the judgment awaiting them and an urgent reminder to the godly of the work needed from them, Jude would lay out several Old Testament examples that would hopefully make his point as plain as day.

DELIVERED AND DESTROYED

Now I want to remind you, although you once fully knew it, that Jesus, who saved a people out of the land of Egypt, afterward destroyed those who did not believe.

JUDE 5 (Emphasis mine)

One of the fun and what might be described as difficult aspects of Jude's Epistle is how often he refers to the Old Testament to make his point. As a lover of the Bible, it forced me to relearn these stories to understand what Jude was trying to communicate. It's easy for Christians to spend all of their time in the New Testament, as if the Old Testament is not also God-breathed, but to have a full grasp of the New Testament you *must* spend time in the Old Testament. So a good amount of our session this week will be reading and looking at Old Testament narratives for the context Jude wants us all to know.

Read the following passages of Scripture, answering the questions for each one.

DELIVERED

ISRAEL IN EGYPT: EXODUS 1:8-14

What did the people of Israel do in Egypt?

How were the people of Israel treated in Egypt?

DELIVERER SENT TO EGYPT: EXODUS 3:7-12

In your own words, what are these verses saying God is going to do and how is He going to do it?

DELIVERED FROM EGYPT: EXODUS 14

How does God deliver Israel from Egypt?

What word is used to describe God's deliverance of Israel? (Hint: see v. 13.)

DESTROYED

Read Numbers 13.

What did God tell Moses to do?

How many spies were sent out?

What bad report did the spies give to Moses, Aaron, and Israel?

What good report did Caleb and Joshua give to the people?

Read Numbers 14:1-38.

How did Israel respond to the bad report by the spies?

What was Caleb and Joshua's reasoning for why Israel shouldn't be afraid?

What word did the Lord use to describe their treatment of Him because of their unbelief in Him (v. 11)?

What was God's judgment on Israel for their unbelief?

God delivered Israel from Egypt in a miraculous and mighty act. Many (really thousands) of some of the same people who were saved from Egypt were destroyed in the wilderness.

What do you think Jude wanted his recipients to understand by using this particular example?

Read 1 Corinthians 10:1-12.

Why did Paul say these things took place?

Behind us is the cross, which provides the only possible escape from the judgment which lies before us. The only way to gain the benefit from that is to believe it now. But there are people in our churches who look and sound like the people of God, but who will not be saved on the last day, because they rebel against God's promises and rule. Like the Israelites in the desert, they do not believe, and in consequence they will face the Judge. That was the case in the wilderness, it was the case in Jude's day, and it will be the case in ours.[1]

DICK LUCAS AND CHRISTOPHER GREEN

Remember, intermingled with Jude's recipients, those he refers to as loved by God, were those who were going unnoticed even though they were living ungodly lives teaching a different "grace" and denying the Lord Jesus. They would've heard Jude's Letter read along with the rest of the group. So the warning was that though they might have been among the people God had saved from destruction, just as the spies and the people who believed them were, they too would be destroyed in like manner if they persisted in their unbelief. Jude was trying to make it very clear that the same Jesus who saves is the same God who will judge.

REJECTING AUTHORITY

> *And the angels who did not stay within their own position of authority,*
> *but left their proper dwelling, he has kept in eternal chains under*
> *gloomy darkness until the judgment of the great day—just as Sodom*
> *and Gomorrah and the surrounding cities, which likewise indulged in*
> *sexual immorality and pursued unnatural desire, serve as an example*
> *by undergoing a punishment of eternal fire.*
>
> **JUDE 6-7**

Jude's second and third examples tell of the rebellion of angels and of the sin of
Sodom and Gomorrah. The first of those, regarding the angels, is a difficult passage
to understand, but passages like these aren't impossible to understand. It will take
some wrestling, searching, reading, and praying, but laboring in God's Word will
always bear more fruit than skimming through God's Word.

**Read verse 6 slowly out loud. It might feel silly, but reading a difficult verse
out loud can assist you in comprehending what's being said.**

What did Jude say the angels did and didn't do?

**Jude described the behavior of the angels and the judgment of God by using
"directional" or "movement" language. I've already circled one example for you.
Circle the other examples.**

*And the angels who did not stay within their own position of authority, but
left their proper dwelling, (he has kept) in eternal chains under gloomy
darkness until the judgment of the great day.*

Remember when Jude referenced being "kept" in Verse 1? Now, he's using kept to describe God's judgment of the angels.

> **What might have Jude wanted his recipients to know by using this theme continually throughout his letter?**

God's ability to keep His own from stumbling shows me how powerful He really is. Both the salvation of His church and the judgment of the ungodly are upheld by Him. To really think about that gives me that much more reverence for him.

At the beginning of verse 5, Jude said he wanted to *remind* his recipients of what they used to know, and he did it by laying out Old Testament stories that would've been familiar to them. In talking about angels that didn't "stay within their own position of authority" (v. 6), Jude was not deviating from his intentions. This too would be a story they'd heard or read before.

Read Genesis 6:1-4.

> **Who are the sons of God? (Hint: Use Job 1:6; 2:1 as references.)**

While there is debate regarding the identity of "the sons of God" in this passage, many scholars agree with the ancient Jewish interpretation stating the sons of God were heavenly beings or angels.[2]

> **Using Jude 5 as your guide, how would you explain what happened in Genesis 6:1-4?**

> **Why was the behavior of the angels considered sin? (See 2 Pet. 2:4.)**

How will they be judged?

Should God have judged them? Why or why not?

Read Genesis 19:1-29.

Why were the angels sent to Sodom?

What observations can you make about the behavior of the people in Sodom? How did these behaviors justify God's destruction of their city?

What two sinful behaviors were present in Sodom and Gomorrah according to Jude? Which verses in Genesis 19 would align with those behaviors?

What do you think Jude meant by "unnatural desire" in verse 7?

How exactly did God judge Sodom and Gomorrah?

The sins of the angels and the people of Sodom and Gomorrah are similar; let's compare them. Mark on the following chart the sins you see present in each.

	PEOPLE OF SODOM & GOMORRAH	ANGELS IN JUDE
Sexual Immorality		
Unnatural desire		
Not staying within their proper place		

Both the rebellious angels and the men of Sodom and Gomorrah sinned against God. Both have and will receive God's judgment. Jude points to the judgment as "the great day" (v. 6).

Read the Scriptures below, noting what each one says about "the great day."

- *Joel 2:1-3*

- *Zephaniah 1:14-16*

- *Malachi 4:1*

- *Revelation 6:12-17*

What is "the great day" Jude was referring to? What will it be like?

Jude said the judgment of Sodom and Gomorrah serves as an example for us. How? Why do you think we need this as an example?

In our culture, we will most likely find ourselves contending for the truth that God is holy and just. Really, God is just because God is holy. A god that isn't concerned with things being right and good wouldn't care about consequences. That kind of god would just shrug his shoulders and ignore injustice in all of its forms. But our God is different because He is holy and eternally incapable of overlooking sin. The God who told Adam and Eve that they would surely die if they ate from the tree is the same God who has told us that the wages of sin is death. Judgment is God's response to sin because sin is our disregard of God's holiness. A holy God must be a just God.

Is it difficult for you to reconcile the fact that God is also judge? If so, why?

Why do you think it's so difficult for us to talk about it with other people?

How might learning about how God will respond to sin compel you to address it?

DAY 3

IGNORANT INSTINCTS

> *Yet in like manner these people also, relying on their dreams, defile the flesh, reject authority, and blaspheme the glorious ones. But when the archangel Michael, contending with the devil, was disputing about the body of Moses, he did not presume to pronounce a blasphemous judgment, but said, "The Lord rebuke you." But these people blaspheme all that they do not understand, and they are destroyed by all that they, like unreasoning animals, understand instinctively.*
>
> **JUDE 8-10**

Jude brought the attention back to the "unnoticed" teachers among them. He said "these people" rely on their dreams (v. 8).

The only other time the Greek term for *dreams (enupniazomai)* is used in the New Testament is in Acts 2:17.3 Read it in your Bible.

What kinds of "dreams" might this be in reference to?

Read Jeremiah 23:25-32. How does God feel about false prophets, specifically those who use their "dreams" to deceive?

If "these people" were perverting God's grace into sensuality (v. 4), how might they have used their claims of having prophetic dreams to do so?

"These people" relying on their dreams were using their supposed revelations from God as the reason why they were defiling the flesh, rejecting authority, and blaspheming angels.

DEFILE THE FLESH

Define:

Defile _____

_____

_____

_____

Flesh can be understood in two ways:
1. Human/Body
2. That which comes from the sinful nature

Look at the passages below and put the corresponding number next to them to indicate which understanding of the flesh is referenced here.

_____ **(1 or 2):** But I say, walk by the Spirit, and you will not gratify the desires of the flesh. —*Galatians 5:16*

_____ **(1 or 2):** And the Word became flesh and dwelt among us, and we have seen his glory, glory as of the only Son from the Father, full of grace and truth. —*John 1:14*

Considering the definition of "the flesh" that's correlated with our sinful nature, Jude can't be saying that they are defiling their sinful nature. Our sinful is nature is already defiled. So what he's addressing is the defilement of the body by these ungodly people.

Read 2 Corinthians 6:14–7:1.

How do you think "these people" were "defiling the flesh"? To find the answer, think about which sin these teachers were engaged in that involves the body.

REJECT AUTHORITY

The Greek word used here for *authority* is *kyriotés* and it means *lordship*.[4] A related word, *kyrios*, was used by Jude many times, including in verse 4.[5]

Circle which word you think it is:

> *For certain people have crept in unnoticed who long ago were designated for this condemnation, ungodly people, who pervert the grace of our God into sensuality and deny our only Master and Lord, Jesus Christ.*
> **JUDE 4**

Who were these people rejecting?

In Week 2, we talked about the different ways one can "deny" Jesus. In their denial, how do you suppose "these people" were rejecting Jesus' authority in their lives? Again, use the examples Jude has given us to shape your answer.

BLASPHEME THE GLORIOUS ONES

To *blaspheme* is to slander or speak evil of something sacred.[6] It seems odd that "these people" would blaspheme the glorious ones (angels) or even that Jude would bring this up as a reason for their condemnation (v. 4). We may not be around many people who make a practice of speaking evil of angels, or maybe we are. But most likely, what Jude is speaking about is harder for us to interpret because there aren't many examples from Scripture on what this might look like.

Jude provides an example for us, although the full story is not present anywhere in Scripture. It is most likely that the following story is one of Jewish tradition that was possibly read and passed along though it never found its way into the canon of Scripture.

When we talk about the canon of Scripture, we're talking about the books of the Old and New Testaments the early church fathers determined as authoritative—inspired by God and profitable for teaching, reproof, correction, and training in righteousness (2 Tim. 3:16). There are 39 canonical books in the Old Testament and 27 in the New Testament.

We're going to look at the story Jude gives us and see how it connects with what he wanted his recipients to know about the character of "these people." But before we do, turn to Deuteronomy 34:1-8 to read what Old Testament Scripture says about the death of Moses.

> *Look at 1:9 and explain in your own words what happened after Moses' death.*

Both Michael and the devil were what?

What didn't Michael do? What did he do?

If Michael was similar to the people Jude was calling out, namely, if he was one to rebel against authority, how different might his response to the devil have been?

Why would Michael, one of the chief angels, appeal to God's authority to rebuke Satan instead of speaking on his own authority?

"These people's" blasphemy of angels being contrasted with Michael's rebuke of the devil leads us to understand that "these people" among them were an irreverent bunch who, unlike Michael, didn't know how to "stay in their place" and live under the authority of God like they were created to do. If angels dare not blaspheme or declare judgment on an evil angel, what will come of human beings that do?

Compare Jude 10 with 2 Peter 2:12.

Jude and 2 Peter were written around the same time to similar audiences. The two resemble one another in style and in content, and some scholars believe Jude used 2 Peter as source material for his Letter.[7]

Both Jude and Peter say that these people blasphemed what they didn't understand, primarily speaking of spiritual things, because of their ignorance at that time. What they did understand and were motivated by was all that they understood instinctively, just like animals.

Instinctively means "naturally."[8] Ephesians 2:1-3 describes how this looks:

> And you were dead in the trespasses and sins in which you once walked, following the course of this world, following the prince of the power of the air, the spirit that is now at work in the sons of disobedience— among whom we all once lived in the passions of our flesh, carrying out the desires of the body and the mind, and were by nature children of wrath, like the rest of mankind.

Letting the verses from Ephesians and the descriptions provided by Jude lead you, what are the instincts of these people leading them to do and what will come of it?

What does this tell you about the primary motivations of false teachers?

What you've learned today is similar to finding the right puzzle pieces to complete a complicated puzzle. So let's put them all together now to see the picture Jude wants us to see. Think through what you learned in today's session. If someone were to ask you to explain verses 8-10, what would you say? (Metaphorically speaking, how would you put the puzzle together?)

DAY 4

WOE

> Woe to them! For they walked in the way of Cain and abandoned themselves for the sake of gain to Balaam's error and perished in Korah's rebellion.
> **JUDE 11**

In the following examples,
1. *Read over the verses that follow, circling each use of the word* woe.
2. *Underline the behavior that's being condemned.*
3. *Put a parenthesis around each judgment.*

OLD TESTAMENT

For the look on their faces bears witness against them; they proclaim their sin like Sodom; they do not hide it. Woe to them! For they have brought evil on themselves. Tell the righteous that it shall be well with them, for they shall eat the fruit of their deeds. Woe to the wicked! It shall be ill with him, for what his hands have dealt out shall be done to him.

ISAIAH 3:9-11

Woe to those who devise wickedness and work evil on their beds! When the morning dawns, they perform it, because it is in the power of their hand. They covet fields and seize them, and houses, and take them away; they oppress a man and his house, a man and his inheritance. Therefore thus says the Lord: behold, against this family I am devising disaster, from which you cannot remove your necks, and you shall not walk haughtily, for it will be a time of disaster.

MICAH 2:1-3

NEW TESTAMENT

And when it was evening, he came with the twelve. And as they were reclining at table and eating, Jesus said, "Truly, I say to you, one of you will betray me, one who is eating with me." They began to be sorrowful and to say to him one after another, "Is it I?" He said to them, "It is one of the twelve, one who is dipping bread into the dish with me. For the Son of Man goes as it is written of him, but woe to that man by whom the Son of Man is betrayed! It would have been better for that man if he had not been born."

MARK 14:17-21

But woe to you who are rich, for you have received your consolation. Woe to you who are full now, for you shall be hungry. Woe to you who laugh now, for you shall mourn and weep. Woe to you, when all people speak well of you, for so their fathers did to the false prophets.

LUKE 6:24-26

Woe to you, scribes and Pharisees, hypocrites! For you build the tombs of the prophets and decorate the monuments of the righteous, saying, "If we had lived in the days of our fathers, we would not have taken part with them in shedding the blood of the prophets." Thus you witness against yourselves that you are sons of those who murdered the prophets. Fill up, then, the measure of your fathers. You serpents, you brood of vipers, how are you to escape being sentenced to hell? Therefore I send you prophets and wise men and scribes, some of whom you will kill and crucify, and some you will flog in your synagogues and persecute from town to town, so that on you may come all the righteous blood shed on earth, from the blood of righteous Abel to the blood of Zechariah the son of Barachiah, whom you murdered between the sanctuary and the altar. Truly, I say to you, all these things will come upon this generation.

MATTHEW 23:29-36

Woe was used often by Old Testament prophets such as Isaiah, Jeremiah, Micah, and Habakkuk. Jesus used the word the most, however, pronouncing judgment on individuals and groups. This word would've been incredibly familiar to Jude's recipients.

Define:

Woe

_____

_____

_____

_____

What do you imagine Jude's readers would have understood and even felt when Jude said "woe to them" to describe "these people" that were going unnoticed among them?

What three Old Testament figures did Jude mention? What adjectives did he use to describe their behavior? (Hint: their behavior corresponds with the behavior of "these people.")

CAIN

Read Genesis 4; Hebrews 11:4; 1 John 3:12-15.

Commentators believe the comparison Jude was trying to make between the ungodly people in their midst and Cain is that of:

1. Hatred/Murder;[9]   2. Disobedience;[10]   3. Self-Centered Worship.[11]

Using the texts listed above along with what Jude has written so far, write out how you think scholars came to those conclusions.

1. Hatred/Murder:

2. Disobedience:

3. Self-Centered Worship:

In your own words, describe "the way of Cain."

BALAAM

Read Numbers 22, paying special attention to the circumstances surrounding Balaam. Glance through chapters 23–24 to see the kind of oracles Balaam spoke to the Moabite king.

Read Numbers 25:1-5.

What did Israel do that brought about God's judgment?

Read Numbers 31:1-3,9-16.

According to Moses, why did Israel sin against God?

Balaam is also mentioned in 2 Peter.

Look up 2 Peter 2:15-16 and read what Peter had to say about him.

Taking all that you've read into account, as well as Jude 11, what are "these people" doing that would make them comparable to Balaam?

KORAH

Read Numbers 16:1-35.

In Jude 4 and 6, Jude gives us clues into the hearts of "these people," showing us they aren't too fond of authority. They'd prefer to be their own masters and similar to the angels, they've left "their proper dwelling" (v. 6).

Where in the story of Korah do you see a refusal to submit to authority?

What does Jude 8 have in common with Numbers 16:1-15? List all you can find.

Why do you think God, through Jude, is trying to emphasize for us what will happen to these people?

When have you had a difficult time submitting to the authority of a teacher, coach, or parent?

JUDE 12-16

As you watch the Week 4 video, answer the following questions:

- What did Enoch warn us would happen?
- Who was going to be judged? What would they be judged for?
- What does God hate? Explain.

After watching the Week 4 video, discuss the following together as a group:

- God is a God of love and He is a judge. Why is it easier to only acknowledge the God of love?
- How has God judged the ungodly in the past?
- How have you seen or experienced God's patience?
- How have you seen God's kindness in your life?

THESE ARE HIDDEN REEFS AT YOUR LOVE FEASTS, AS THEY FEAST WITH YOU WITHOUT FEAR, SHEPHERDS FEEDING THEMSELVES; WATERLESS CLOUDS, SWEPT ALONG BY WINDS; FRUITLESS TREES IN LATE AUTUMN, TWICE DEAD, UPROOTED; 13WILD WAVES OF THE SEA, CASTING UP THE FOAM OF THEIR OWN SHAME; WANDERING STARS, FOR WHOM THE GLOOM OF UTTER DARKNESS HAS BEEN RESERVED FOREVER.

14IT WAS ALSO ABOUT THESE THAT ENOCH, THE SEVENTH FROM ADAM, PROPHESIED, SAYING, "BEHOLD, THE LORD COMES WITH TEN THOUSANDS OF HIS HOLY ONES, 15TO EXECUTE JUDGMENT ON ALL AND TO CONVICT ALL THE UNGODLY OF ALL THEIR DEEDS OF UNGODLINESS THAT THEY HAVE COMMITTED IN SUCH AN UNGODLY WAY, AND OF ALL THE HARSH THINGS THAT UNGODLY SINNERS HAVE SPOKEN AGAINST HIM." 16THESE ARE GRUMBLERS, MALCONTENTS, FOLLOWING THEIR OWN SINFUL DESIRES; THEY ARE LOUD-MOUTHED BOASTERS, SHOWING FAVORITISM TO GAIN ADVANTAGE.

JUDE 12-16

Continuing in his descriptions of the ungodly men hiding among God's people, Jude used nature to help his recipients further understand how these men behaved, finally concluding this portion of his letter by explaining what will become of these men once they stand before God. Jude was not afraid to speak about the immoral behavior of these men nor did he mince words when writing about the judgment awaiting them. We might be in a culture that prefers a "love" that doesn't address sin, hell, and holiness. But Jude, just like his master and Lord, Jesus, must tell the truth, even if it's difficult for others to hear.

WATERLESS CLOUDS & FRUITLESS TREES

> *These are hidden reefs at your love feasts, as they feast with you without fear, shepherds feeding themselves; waterless clouds, swept along by winds; fruitless trees in late autumn, twice dead, uprooted; wild waves of the sea, casting up the foam of their own shame; wandering stars, for whom the gloom of utter darkness has been reserved forever.*
>
> **JUDE 12-13**

HIDDEN REEFS AT YOUR LOVE FEASTS, AS THEY FEAST WITH YOU WITHOUT FEAR

What's your initial thought as to what Jude might have been saying about "these people" with this description?

Look at the Greek definition of the word "reefs" below:

spilas:
Original Word: σπιλάς, άδος, ἡ
Part of Speech: Noun, Feminine
Transliteration: spilas
Phonetic Spelling: (spee-las')
Definition: a ledge of rock (over which the sea dashes), a reef
Usage: a hidden rock; fig: a flaw, stigma[1]
STRONG'S CONCORDANCE

Reefs give the imagery of a rock that's hidden in the sea and dangerous to any ship that would get too close to it.

Taking into consideration that definition, in Jude comparing these men to "reefs," what was he saying they were to the Christian community?

SHEPHERDS FEEDING THEMSELVES

What's your initial thought as to what Jude might have been saying about "these people" with this description?

Read the passage below and underline the actions of *selfish* shepherds.

> *The word of the LORD came to me: "Son of man, prophesy against the shepherds of Israel; prophesy, and say to them, even to the shepherds, Thus says the Lord GOD: Ah, shepherds of Israel who have been feeding yourselves! Should not shepherds feed the sheep? You eat the fat, you clothe yourselves with the wool, you slaughter the fat ones, but you do not feed the sheep. The weak you have not strengthened, the sick you have not healed, the injured you have not bound up, the strayed you have not brought back, the lost you have not sought, and with force and harshness you have ruled them."*
> **EZEKIEL 34:1-4**

Read the passage below and underline the actions of a *humble* shepherd.

> *So I exhort the elders among you, as a fellow elder and a witness of the sufferings of Christ, as well as a partaker in the glory that is going to be revealed: shepherd the flock of God that is among you, exercising oversight, not under compulsion, but willingly, as God would have you; not for shameful gain, but eagerly; not domineering over those in your charge, but being examples to the flock. And when the chief Shepherd appears, you will receive the unfading crown of glory.*
> **1 PETER 5:1-4**

Jude was referencing Ezekiel when he condemned "these people" for being shepherds who are feeding themselves. What should we as God's beloved people be able to observe about similar people in our own churches by considering this description?

WATERLESS CLOUDS, SWEPT ALONG BY WINDS; FRUITLESS TREES IN LATE AUTUMN, TWICE DEAD, UPROOTED

What's your initial thought as to what Jude might have been saying about "these people" with this description?

Read Proverbs 25:14.

These men were like waterless clouds, presenting themselves as having something they couldn't give and promising something that their words couldn't provide.

One thing I've heard many, many times is the idea that because God is love, I shouldn't worry about God's judgment. The empty promise is that I'd escape God's wrath even if I never repented of my particular sins. The waterless clouds that have said this believe they are delivering me and others truth—a truth that should free us. But instead of freedom, this kind of message only delivers slavery.

Do you have an example of when you've heard teaching that can be described as coming from a "waterless cloud"? Explain.

Jude's descriptions of these ungodly people are relevant. We too are surrounded by teachers that are terrible guides, seemingly impressive in their presentation but fruitless in their character. Offering us all a pathway to freedom that will only end in death. It's difficult to discern the reality of who these people are when we like how they say what they say instead of listening to what they're saying. God's Word really is a lamp unto our feet, by learning it and following it, we won't be led astray.

What might the metaphor of them being "fruitless trees" tell us about "these people"? And what parable (hint, hint) did Jesus share in Luke (hint, hint) that would give us more insight on how to understand Jude's description here?

As clouds without rain, they are being swept along by the wind. As trees without fruit, they are twice dead, uprooted.

What does that say about the stability of "these people" and the expected condemnation for "these people"?

WILD WAVES OF THE SEA, CASTING UP THE FOAM OF THEIR OWN SHAME; WANDERING STARS, FOR WHOM THE GLOOM OF UTTER DARKNESS HAS BEEN RESERVED FOREVER

What's your initial thought as to what Jude might have been saying about "these people" with this description?

Read Isaiah 57:20.

If you've ever been to a beach, you have most likely seen how wild the ocean can be. When the waves move toward the sand, it's loud, sometimes big, sometimes small, but it's hard to miss the ocean's movement. It's noticeable and impressive to most. At first glance, the waves look nice and clean until you see them retreat and all that's left on the sand is whatever dirt, sticks, and messiness was hidden inside of it.

So a wandering star provides a neat image for a deceptive leadership that promises security and a safe road home, but actually delivers uncertainty and danger. The longer the traveller believed in the certainty of his wandering star, the greater the peril he was in. The ultimate wandering star is the great deceiver himself, the fallen star called Satan. Many New Testament writers warn of the deceptive danger of false teaching, but Jude's warning has a particular power reinforced by a connection hard to see in English. He has warned of "Balaam's error" (plane, verse 11) and now warns of the wandering (*planetes*) that the error produces.[2]

DICK LUCAS AND CHRISTOPHER GREEN

If these teachers were like the ocean in all of their pomp and supposed beauty that was noticed by onlookers, what was Jude saying will actually come of all that they did? And how should it inform the way we think about whatever it is that they say?

They are also called "wandering stars." Before there were GPS systems on our phones and radar systems set in place to direct people on where to go, the stars were a guide.

In your own words, explain why following a wandering star would be dangerous.

What is the judgment awaiting them, and what group did Jude mention earlier awaiting the same fate?

What four elements of nature does Jude use to describe the ungodly teachers?

HELL

> It was also about these that Enoch, the seventh from Adam, prophesied, saying, "Behold, the Lord comes with ten thousands of his holy ones, to execute judgment on all and to convict all the ungodly of all their deeds of ungodliness that they have committed in such an ungodly way, and of all the harsh things that ungodly sinners have spoken against him." These are grumblers, malcontents, following their own sinful desires; they are loud-mouthed boasters, showing favoritism to gain advantage.
>
> **JUDE 14-16**

Jude continued in this theme of using narratives and people from the past to make a point for those he was writing to presently, so that they'd be aware of what was going to happen in the future.

Why do God's words and the examples of God's judgment in the past matter for us today?

What influence do they have over how and why we'll contend for the faith?

What does Hebrews 11:5 tell us about Enoch?

Jude has mentioned "the Lord" at other times in his Epistle. See the following list of verses and the corresponding traits.

> **Verse 4:** The Lord is our only Master and Lord.
> **Verse 8:** The Lord rebukes.

Now in verses 14-15, this same Lord executes judgment.

Read Matthew 16:27; 25:31; and Luke 9:26.

> *Who is coming with ten thousands of His holy ones?*

Now read John 5:22-29.

> *This understanding of Jesus as the Lord who will execute judgment on the ungodly isn't thought of often by many Christians or even taught often in some pulpits. Why do you think that is?*

God's judgment of the ungodly will culminate in them being thrown into fiery furnace (Matt. 13:41-42), which is also known as "hell."

In the New Testament, Jesus spoke about hell the most. It is the loving Son of God, Jesus Christ, who provided descriptions for us to understand what hell (a.k.a. the place where God's divine wrath will be eternally poured out on the ungodly) will be like.

People commonly push back against the doctrine of hell, saying it seems like a contradiction for God to be considered loving and yet send people to hell. "If God is love," they say, "no one should go to hell."

> *If someone were to ask you, "How can a loving God send people to hell?" what would you say in the defense of the truth (or the faith)?*

God is love but God is also holy. It is because He is loving that He must also hate.

Read the verses below in your own Bible. Beside each passage write down what it says God hates:

- *Psalm 5:5*

- *Psalm 11:5*

- *Proverbs 6:16-19*

> For you are not a God who delights in wickedness;
> evil may not dwell with you.
> **PSALM 5:4**

> They still bear fruit in old age; they are ever full of sap and green, to declare that the LORD is upright; he is my rock, and there is no unrighteousness in him.
> **PSALM 92:14-15**

> You know that he appeared in order to take away sins, and in him there is no sin.
> **1 JOHN 3:5**

Do you think there is a connection between the holiness of God and His hatred of sin? Why or why not?

God is love. God is holy. And God is also just.

> For the wrongdoer will be paid back
> for the wrong he has done, and there
> is no partiality.
> **COLOSSIANS 3:25**

Imagine if we lived in a world where all sins against God and people, such as lying, stealing, adultery, murder, racism, sexual immorality, and abuse, just to name a few, were never dealt with.

Imagine if we had a justice system that never executed justice. Where those who have murdered were not indicted. Where those who have stolen millions were not caught and kept from doing the same thing again. Where those who have abused the vulnerable, oppressed the poor, and failed to care for the marginalized were never ever confronted about their wrongdoing. At a fundamental level, we'd conclude that a justice system like that was unjust and if unjust, then not *good*.

This might describe our current justice system and the world in which we live, but it does not and will never describe God. God's holy goodness means He must judge all wrongdoing. No matter how big or small.

> For love to be truly loving, there must be judgment. If there is no judgment, then there is no hope for a slave, a rape victim, a child who has been abused or bullied, or people who have been slandered or robbed or had their dignity stolen. If nobody is called to account before a cosmic judgment seat for violence and oppression, then the victims will never see justice. We need a God who gets angry. We need a God who will protect his kids, who will once and for all remove bullies and perpetrators of evil from his playground.[3]
>
> **SCOTT SAULS**

How does God's justice better help you understand His love?

Close today in prayer, thanking God for His love, His goodness, and His justice.

UNGODLY

> It was also about these that Enoch, the seventh from Adam, prophesied, saying, "Behold, the Lord comes with ten thousands of his holy ones, to execute judgment on all and to convict all the ungodly of all their deeds of ungodliness that they have committed in such an ungodly way, and of all the harsh things that ungodly sinners have spoken against him." These are grumblers, malcontents, following their own sinful desires; they are loud-mouthed boasters, showing favoritism to gain advantage.
>
> **JUDE 14-16**

In the above verses,
1. *Circle every use of the word* **all.**
2. *Underline every use of the word* **ungodly.**

What might Jude have been trying to communicate with the repetition of both words in these verses?

In verse 4, Jude also made a reference to the ungodly. Who was he talking about then that clues us in on who he's talking about now?

What two things will the ungodly be judged for according to verse 15?

What did the previous verses in Jude say the ungodly will be judged for?

Taking into account the character of God, why might these deeds be considered "ungodly"?

For example: The self-centeredness of being shepherds that only feed themselves (v. 12) is completely antithetical to God who is the Good Shepherd. As Psalm 23 puts it, the Lord leads us, comforts us, and restores us. His shepherding of us is in service to us—unlike the shepherds which Jude condemns.

Read Matthew 12:33-37.

Jesus' words in Matthew confirm Enoch's prophecy as quoted by Jude.

Following Jude's train of thought into verse 16, put a star next to each example in the verses at the top of page 94 of the ungodly men's words.

Read 1 Corinthians 10:6-11.

In what verse does Paul talk about grumblers? What Old Testament story is he referencing? (Hint: Jude referenced the same Old Testament story early on in his Epistle.)

Read Numbers 13:30-33; 14:1-4.

Unbelieving Israel grumbled (complained) to Moses and Aaron after the ten spies came back and told them they'd be unable to take the land even though God had previously promised He'd *give* it to them (Gen. 15:18-19).

In their grumbling, they were more willing to be slaves again in Egypt than to trust God in the wilderness. They also chose not to listen to the authorities God set over them (Moses and Aaron) and decided to do what *they* thought best.

> *If "these men" (Jude 8) were denying the authority of Jesus, what might they have grumbled about concerning Jesus? For example, one possibility is that they grumbled by saying, "Jesus' commands are just too restrictive. What kind of a God would force people to obey Him in everything?"*

> *If "these men" were perverting God's grace, what might they have grumbled about concerning God's commands?*

> **mempsimoiros:**
> *Original Word:* μεμψίμοιρος, ον
> *Part of Speech:* Adjective
> *Transliteration:* mempsimoiros
> *Phonetic Spelling:* (mem-psim'-oy-ros)
> *Definition:* complaining of one's fate
> *Usage:* blaming one's lot or destiny, discontented, complaining.[4]

Naturally, discontentment partners with grumbling. Where there is one, the other will follow.

> *How does dissatisfaction in the person of God affect submission to the Word of God?*

Have you ever been discontent with where God has you or what God has told you and it's led you to "grumble" against Him? Explain.

In that way, we can all relate to what these teachers are being accused of. However, being unlike them because of salvation, the godly (beloved) are not slaves to unbelief as they once were. So even if there are seasons of grumbling and discontentment, they don't last forever.

One surefire way to identify these ungodly men is by asking the questions,"Do they complain about God's Word more than they submit to it?" "Are they content with serving God as He has commanded to be served or are they always coming up with alternative ways to *look* obedient?"

The behavior and character of "these men" has been communicated in great detail, but what is it that is controlling these men that leads them to live as they do? (Look up Jas. 1:14-15 for greater clarity on how to answer.)

But these people blaspheme all that they do not understand, and they are destroyed by all that they, like unreasoning animals, understand instinctively.
JUDE 10

For the time is coming when people will not endure sound teaching, but having itching ears they will accumulate for themselves teachers to suit their own passions.
2 TIMOTHY 4:3

These are grumblers, malcontents, following their own sinful desires.
JUDE 16a

" … understand instinctively."
" … their own passions."
" … their own sinful desires."

What do all three of these descriptions have in common?
Sinful desires shape *how* these men live.
Sinful desires shape *why* these men are believed.
Sinful desires shape *what* controls these men.

Compare Jude 16 with 2 Peter 2:18.

Jude says that these men are "loud-mouthed boasters." Peter says the men he's addressing in his letter speak with "loud boasts of folly." What do you think they were trying to communicate about the arrogance of these men and how it came out in their speech?

In their grandiose speech and fanciful language, these men use both to flatter others so that they can take advantage of them or their resources.

Is partiality (favoritism) sinful? Why or why not? Use Scripture to defend your position.

> But you have turned aside from the way. You have caused many to stumble by your instruction. You have corrupted the covenant of Levi, says the Lord of hosts, and so I make you despised and abased before all the people, inasmuch as you do not keep my ways but show partiality in your instruction.
> **MALACHI 2:8-9**

What do you think it would've looked like for the priests in Malachi to show "partiality in [their] instruction" (v. 9) and how might it have looked for these ungodly men to do the same?

How could their partiality be advantageous to them? What would they have had to gain, in a worldly sense, from telling people they could sin freely?

In Matthew 16:24, Jesus said, "If anyone would come after me, let him deny himself and take up his cross and follow me."

In Romans 8:13, Paul said, "For if you live according to the flesh you will die, but if by the Spirit you put to death the deeds of the body, you will live."

In 1 Peter 2:11, Peter said, "Beloved, I urge you as sojourners and exiles to abstain from the passions of the flesh, which wage war against your soul."

In 1 John 3:6, John said, "No one who abides in him keeps on sinning; no one who keeps on sinning has either seen him or known him."

What would these teachers have had to lose by teaching what Jesus and His apostles taught?

Being partial in our instruction would make contending for the faith much easier considering the volatile society we're in. The preservation of our own comforts and the privileges afforded to preaching a half gospel can make it tempting to lay aside what we know to be true. There's a lot to lose when preaching the entire gospel. The gospel that doesn't only say "You aren't condemned" but includes "Go and sin no more" (John 8:11). We can lose friends, jobs, followers, esteem, and so on.

Have you "lost" anything for being faithful to Scripture?

Be encouraged by this word:

> *Now who is there to harm you if you are zealous for what is good? But even if you should suffer for righteousness' sake, you will be blessed. Have no fear of them, nor be troubled, but in your hearts honor Christ the Lord as holy, always being prepared to make a defense to anyone who asks you for a reason for the hope that is in you; yet do it with gentleness and respect, having a good conscience, so that, when you are slandered, those who revile your good behavior in Christ may be put to shame. For it is better to suffer for doing good, if that should be God's will, than for doing evil.*
>
> **1 PETER 3:13-16**

DAY 4

PRAY

During the last two weeks of our study, we spent a considerable amount of time learning more about God's wrath—what it looks like, when it will come, and who it will come to. If you were like me while studying this portion of Jude's Letter, by the end, you might have felt the weight of it all. The judgment of God is real, and there are millions of people who are woefully ignorant to its reality.

There are also Christians, who may or may not be theologically equipped to understand God's wrath, that because of timidity, will refrain from addressing the topic. The fear of man often motivates their "gospel" presentations more than the fear of God, and because of this, people are not being warned as to why they must repent and believe.

If we're honest, all of us, including me, have behaved this way. Whether it was with an unbelieving friend, classmate, or family member, we've all shrunk back from saying the difficult thing because we were afraid of how it would be received. So I think that

today, we should pray. Pray for the people we personally know who are blind to that "great day" and the all-consuming fire that is God (Heb. 12:29). And pray for ourselves, that God would give us the courage to tell them the truth, the whole truth, when the opportunity is made available.

> *Write down the names of the people you want to pray for. Spend time on each name, praying God would grant repentance, leading to a knowledge of the truth (1 Tim. 2:4) and whatever else you sense the Holy Spirit leading you to pray (Jude 20).*

1.

2.

3.

4.

Keeping your relationship with each person in mind, pray that God would open up a door for you to share His Word (Col. 4:3-4) and to declare Christ to them. Pray you'd do it *clearly* and *courageously* (Acts 4:23-31).

JUDE 17-23

As you watch the Week 5 video, answer the following questions:

- In which verse did Jude first refer to his recipients as "beloved"?
- List the four essential aspects of the Christian faith that will guard against false teaching and equip us to contend.
- How are we to pray?
- What does Jude command of recipients in these verses?

After watching the Week 5 video, discuss the following together as a group:

- Why does Jude address how his recipients should live before identifying how they should respond to false teachers?
- How have you built a firm foundation of Christian faith in your life? Who helped you to lay this foundation?
- How is God's salvation evident in your past, present, and future?
- How can keeping your sights on the rewards of heaven and the hope of Jesus Christ protect you from temptations of false teachings?

BUT YOU MUST REMEMBER, BELOVED, THE PREDICTIONS OF THE APOSTLES OF OUR LORD JESUS CHRIST. [18]THEY SAID TO YOU, "IN THE LAST TIME THERE WILL BE SCOFFERS, FOLLOWING THEIR OWN UNGODLY PASSIONS." [19]IT IS THESE WHO CAUSE DIVISIONS, WORLDLY PEOPLE, DEVOID OF THE SPIRIT. [20]BUT YOU, BELOVED, BUILDING YOURSELVES UP IN YOUR MOST HOLY FAITH AND PRAYING IN THE HOLY SPIRIT, [21]KEEP YOURSELVES IN THE LOVE OF GOD, WAITING FOR THE MERCY OF OUR LORD JESUS CHRIST THAT LEADS TO ETERNAL LIFE. [22]AND HAVE MERCY ON THOSE WHO DOUBT; [23]SAVE OTHERS BY SNATCHING THEM OUT OF THE FIRE; TO OTHERS SHOW MERCY WITH FEAR, HATING EVEN THE GARMENT STAINED BY THE FLESH.

JUDE 17-23

In the beginning of Jude's Letter, he told his recipients he wanted them to contend for the faith, but he didn't detail how until now. Before he provided them instructions for contending, he exhorted them in what will grow them in their character—because contending for the faith is as much about living and growing in the faith as it is defending it. Being grounded in the Scriptures and growing in faith toward God is what keeps the feet of any Christian from shifting when the wind from sinful living and teaching blows their way.

REMEMBER

> *But you must remember, beloved, the predictions of the apostles of our Lord Jesus Christ. They said to you, "In the last time there will be scoffers, following their own ungodly passions." It is these who cause divisions, worldly people, devoid of the Spirit*
> **JUDE 17-19**

In what earlier verse does Jude bring up the act of "remembering"?

By wanting them to remember the predictions (prophecies) of the apostles, Jude is landing the plane on apostolic authority. The Old Testament contained examples for them of what to expect. Enoch prophesied, warning them and others of what to expect. And the apostles prophesied, which if Jude's recipients remembered their words, Jude's Epistle shouldn't come as a shock, but rather a confirmation that what God has continually said would happen, is happening.

Underline what these verses say will come in the last days:

> *But understand this, that in the last days there will come times of difficulty.*
> **2 TIMOTHY 3:1**

> *I am stirring up your sincere mind by way of reminder, that you should remember the predictions of the holy prophets and the commandment of the Lord and Savior through your apostles, knowing this first of all, that scoffers will come in the last days with scoffing, following their own sinful desires.*
> **2 PETER 3:1a-3**

> *Now the Spirit expressly says that in later times some will depart from the faith by devoting themselves to deceitful spirits and teachings of demons.*
>
> **1 TIMOTHY 4:1**

> *But false prophets also arose among the people, just as there will be false teachers among you, who will secretly bring in destructive heresies, even denying the Master who bought them, bringing upon themselves swift destruction.*
>
> **2 PETER 2:1**

ESCHATOLOGY: study of the end times

Have you ever known someone who would be considered a "scoffer" or who was bringing "heresies" into the church? If so, what does that tell you about how you should understand "the last days"?

Read Psalm 1:1 in your Bible and define its use of the word scoffer (or mocker depending on your translation).

Read Psalm 42:10,79:9-10, and Jeremiah 17:14-15.

What question characterizes scoffers?

Read 2 Peter 3:3-7.

What were the scoffers questioning in Peter's Letter?

This behavior is present in the ungodly men Jude has been trying to call out. They are a skeptical bunch who won't flat out deny the existence of God, but they will mock the Word of God and the promises of God, especially regarding His coming judgment. Perhaps that's why Jude spent so much time using past narratives to point to a future reality—giving the scoffers ample opportunity to see that God had not returned in judgment yet because He was actually being patient toward them.

> But do not overlook this one fact, beloved, that with the Lord one day is as a thousand years, and a thousand years as one day. The Lord is not slow to fulfill his promise as some count slowness, but is patient toward you, not wishing that any should perish, but that all should reach repentance.
>
> **2 PETER 3:8-9**

Some "mockers" can present themselves as being on the intellectual side of things, sometimes providing "biblical evidence" to support their conclusions. Look at Jude verses 10,16,18. Had "these people" come to believe what they believed and teach what they taught because of proper biblical interpretation or was there some other hidden motivation at work? Explain how you came to that conclusion.

Do not underestimate the influence of one's passions on one's biblical interpretation. These people were not perverting grace, blaspheming angels, and seducing others to sin because they'd found a rare and supposedly right interpretation of Scripture. They weren't enlightened. Their hearts were darkened (Eph. 4:18), which led them to manipulate God's Word for wicked means.

Read John 17:20-23.

How many times does Jesus pray that Christians would be one? Why does He pray for that?

I therefore, a prisoner for the Lord, urge you to walk in a manner worthy of the calling to which you have been called, with all humility and gentleness, with patience, bearing with one another in love, eager to maintain the unity of the Spirit in the bond of peace. There is one body and one Spirit—just as you were called to the one hope that belongs to your call—one Lord, one faith, one baptism, one God and Father of all, who is over all and through all and in all.

EPHESIANS 4:1-6

Read the verses above and open up your Bible to Galatians 5:22-23. Looking at both, who must Christians be led by to walk in the unity for which Jesus prayed?

Looking at Jude 19, do these men have what Galatians 5:22-23 produces?

Jude has made a strong case for how ungodly "these men" are throughout his entire Letter, and if his recipients needed a bit more clarity, he told them that they are "devoid of the spirit" (v. 19). It makes sense, then, why they were causing divisions. "These people" didn't want Christians to be one because if they were, they'd be following Jesus and not them. These people had introduced particular doctrines and flattered particular people, causing divisions in the church, but in God's providence, by Him using Jude to call this division to their attention, the church will be able to purge themselves of the evil unnoticed among them (1 Cor. 5:12-13), thus allowing them to continue in the unity Jesus prayed God would preserve.

DAY 2

KEEP YOURSELVES IN THE LOVE OF GOD

> *But you, beloved, building yourselves up in your most holy faith and praying in the Holy Spirit, keep yourselves in the love of God, waiting for the mercy of our Lord Jesus Christ that leads to eternal life.*
>
> **JUDE 20-21**

These verses use language from the first three verses of Jude. Fill out the chart below with the corresponding terms in the verses above.

TERM IN VERSES 1-3	TERM IN VERSES 20-21
Kept (for Jesus)	_____ (yourselves).
Loved (by God)	_____ of God
Mercy	_____ (of Jesus)
Beloved	But you, _____
Faith (once for all delivered)	(Most holy) _____

We often talk about two moods of speech when we talk about the Epistles in Scripture: imperative and indicative. Indicative statements are factual statements; you're indicating that something is true. Imperative statements are commands or requests. The Epistles have both.

In Jude 20-21, what is the imperative statement?

The imperative or primary command is: "keep yourselves in the love of God" (v. 21). The other three "clauses" or phrases in verses 20-21 are Jude's instruction on how they can keep themselves in the love of God.

BUILDING YOURSELVES UP IN YOUR MOST HOLY FAITH

Look back at Week 2 (p. 47) and consider how our definition of faith from verse 3 applies to the "most holy faith" in verse 20.

How do you personally build yourself up in the faith?

The metaphor of Christians building something or being built upon or into something is common in the New Testament.

Read the verses below:

1 CORINTHIANS 3:10-11

What is the foundation on which the church (Christians) are built on?

EPHESIANS 2:19-22

How is the structure (which is representative of many Christians and not one Christian, emphasizing the unity that exists between them) growing and for what reason?

COLOSSIANS 2:6-7

If you received Jesus Christ by faith, which rooted you, what might it look to grow or be built up in Him?

Read the verse below and underline how the early church built themselves up in the faith.

And they devoted themselves to the apostles' teaching and the fellowship, to the breaking of bread and the prayers.

ACTS 2:42

How have you experienced being built up by devoting yourself to the apostles' teaching?

How have you experienced being built up by being in a community of believers where there is fellowship and the breaking of bread (sharing a meal with other Christians)?

What changes or consequences have you seen in yourself or others as a result of choosing isolation over fellowship with other believers?

How have you experienced being built up by praying with other believers?

Being built up in the faith seems to have a whole lot to do with Jesus, faith, and community—all of which the unnoticed teachers cared nothing about. They were denying Jesus; they were unbelieving; and they were divisive. But Jude's recipients were being reminded to continue to trust Jesus, His character and His Word, for that would build them up. He was reminding them to do this alongside other Christians (building yourselves up in your most holy faith) because together they would build each other up. Christians who were intentional about building themselves up in the faith would not be easily swayed by "these men," for they would be a part of a building that was stable, one that the wind could not sway because its foundation was not made of sand like what these men stood on. God's beloved had a sturdy footing because their foundation was Jesus Himself.

PRAYING IN THE HOLY SPIRIT

The ungodly men in Jude's Letter were "devoid of the Spirit" (v. 19), but now that Jude had returned to speaking about and to those who are called, beloved, and kept, his appeal was for them to pray how all godly people should pray and how all godly people *can* pray.

> **What comes to your mind when you read the words "praying in the Holy Spirit" (v. 20)?**

The Holy Spirit leads us in how we speak.

> *Therefore I want you to understand that no one speaking in the Spirit of God ever says "Jesus is accursed!" and no one can say "Jesus is Lord" except in the Holy Spirit.*
> **1 CORINTHIANS 12:3**

The Holy Spirit leads us in how we live.

> *But if you are led by the Spirit, you are not under the law.*
> **GALATIANS 5:18**

The Holy Spirit leads us in how we address God.

> For you did not receive the spirit of slavery to fall back into fear, but you have
> received the Spirit of adoption as sons, by whom we cry, "Abba! Father!"
> **ROMANS 8:15**

Thinking about how being in and led by the Holy Spirit determines how we speak, live, and relate to God, what do you think Jude was saying in telling them to "[pray] in the Holy Spirit" (v. 20)? (Read Rom. 8:26 for a little more help.)

Prayer is a struggle for all Christians because dependence is a struggle for all people. It's difficult for us to pray simply because it's difficult for us to remember how much we need God. Jude's appeal for them to pray in the Holy Spirit would have made them a people who didn't depend on themselves or their intellect or aging wisdom to figure out everything. They could've been similar to us in that while building themselves up in the faith, maybe by studying biblical doctrine or by being busy in ministry, they'd soon forgotten that knowing a lot about God shouldn't make you more independent of God. Jude wanted them to be a group of needy people that would be led by the Spirit in how they lived and how they prayed.

How do you think praying in the Spirit should shape how we pray?

Think about how often you pray. Consider your disposition in prayer too. Are you falling asleep? Easily distracted? Is your prayer directed to God or for praise? Are you doing it to check off a box on your Christian to-do list? Is it vulnerable? Fabricated? These are all questions worth considering as you read over the following verses.

> And when you pray, do not heap up empty phrases as the Gentiles do, for
> they think that they will be heard for their many words.
> **MATTHEW 6:7**

> *Pray at all times in the Spirit with every prayer and request, and stay alert with all perseverance and intercession for all the saints.*
>
> **EPHESIANS 6:18, CSB**

> *And when you pray, you must not be like the hypocrites. For they love to stand and pray in the synagogues and at the street corners, that they may be seen by others. Truly, I say to you, they have received their reward. But when you pray, go into your room and shut the door and pray to your Father who is in secret.*
>
> **MATTHEW 6:5-6a**

> *Pray without ceasing.*
>
> **1 THESSALONIANS 5:17**

What aspect of praying in the Spirit included in the verses we've just read do you struggle with the most?

How do you think praying in the Spirit should shape what we pray?

Think about the content of your prayers. Are they shaped by Scripture? In consideration of today and eternity? Do they include your deepest worries and fears for yourself as well as others? Do you pray for the people around you who are struggling as well as the people around you who are growing? Do they include all people or only people you like? Relate to? Agree with? Are your prayers thankful? Do they contain praise? Consider these questions as you read over the following below:

> *First of all, then, I urge that supplications, prayers, intercessions, and thanksgivings be made for all people.*
>
> **1 TIMOTHY 2:1**

For this reason I bow my knees before the Father, from whom every family in heaven and on earth is named, that according to the riches of his glory he may grant you to be strengthened with power through his Spirit in your inner being, so that Christ may dwell in your hearts through faith—that you, being rooted and grounded in love, may have strength to comprehend with all the saints what is the breadth and length and height and depth, and to know the love of Christ that surpasses knowledge, that you may be filled with all the fullness of God.

EPHESIANS 3:14-19

Do not be anxious about anything, but in everything by prayer and supplication with thanksgiving let your requests be made known to God.

PHILIPPIANS 4:6

Pray then like this: "Our Father in heaven, hallowed be your name. Your kingdom come, your will be done, on earth as it is in heaven. Give us this day our daily bread, and forgive us our debts, as we also have forgiven our debtors. And lead us not into temptation, but deliver us from evil.

MATTHEW 6:9-13

What aspect of praying in the Spirit included in the verses we've just read do you struggle with the most?

Now, put your pen down, put your phone or whatever element of distraction is nearby to the side and pray in the Spirit.

Whatever aspect of praying in the Spirit you struggle with, whether it's how you pray or for what you pray, talk to God about it. Take your time, too. It's a conversation, not a race. God is in heaven listening to you, His Son is beside Him interceding for you, and the Spirit is inside of you ready to guide you.

KEEP YOURSELVES IN THE LOVE OF GOD

> *But you, beloved, building yourselves up in your most holy faith and praying in the Holy Spirit, keep yourselves in the love of God, waiting for the mercy of our Lord Jesus Christ that leads to eternal life.*
>
> **JUDE 20-21**

For Jude's recipients, "keep yourselves in the love of God" is the primary command from Jude here and the other sentences are instructions on how they'd be able to keep themselves in the love of God. For that reason, we will study the instruction to wait for the mercy of the Lord Jesus first before seeing how all of these individual exhortations work together to accomplish the primary one.

WAITING FOR THE MERCY OF OUR LORD JESUS CHRIST

Where have we seen the word mercy *before and what did we learn about its meaning?*

Awaiting mercy might seem like an odd thing to do if we have already received mercy (Titus 3:5, Rom. 12:1).

One way to understand what Jude means is to answer this question: When Jesus comes back, we fully expect and believe that the ungodly will receive eternal condemnation (Jude 4,7,11,13,14,15), but when Jesus returns, what should the godly expect to receive?

Read Romans 5:9-10 in your Bible and answer the question below:

God's wrath and final judgment on the ungodly is a future reality. According to this verse, what will salvation look like for those who have been justified?

> *For they themselves report concerning us the kind of reception we had among you, and how you turned to God from idols to serve the living and true God, and to wait for his Son from heaven, whom he raised from the dead, Jesus who delivers us from the wrath to come.*
>
> **1 THESSALONIANS 1:9-10**

In the passage above:
1. **Circle the word "wait"**
2. **Draw an arrow toward the object of their waiting**
3. **Underline the timing of God's wrath**

Keeping Romans 5:9-10 and 1 Thessalonians 1:9-10 in mind, what does it mean to "wait for mercy"?

The mercy we are waiting for leads to eternal life. John 3:16, everybody's favorite verse, points to this truth.

Turn to John 3:16 in your Bible and look at the words "eternal life." Who will receive it?

What is eternal life contrasted with?

Jude wanted his recipients to be a hopeful people always looking forward, living with and anchored by a real and tangible hope. Similar to Moses who "... considered the reproach of Christ greater wealth than the treasures of Egypt, for he was looking to the reward" (Heb. 11:26).

Or of other men and women in the hall of fame of faith about whom was said:

> "These all died in faith, not having received the things promised, but having seen them and greeted them from afar, and having acknowledged that they were strangers and exiles on the earth. For people who speak thus make it clear that they are seeking a homeland. If they had been thinking of that land from which they had gone out, they would have had opportunity to return. But as it is, they desire a better country, that is, a heavenly one. Therefore God is not ashamed to be called their God, for he has prepared for them a city."
>
> **HEBREWS 11:13-16**

It must have been an encouragement for Jude's recipients to be challenged to wait for mercy—looking toward their eschatological hope especially after spending a significant amount of time being warned of the condemnation awaiting the ungodly teachers among them. They too, the godly that is, are told about their future. And it is truly a glorious one.

KEEP YOURSELVES IN THE LOVE OF GOD

Where has Jude used the word "love" before and what did we learn about it?

Jude has been using the word "kept" all throughout his Letter.

How does the first use of the word kept and the last use of the word kept inform how you think about the command to "keep [yourself] in the love of God" (v. 21)?

> *As the Father has loved me, so have I loved you. Abide in my love.*
> **JOHN 15:9**

Do you think Jesus' words above are similar to Jude's words in verse 21? Why or why not?

You might be wondering this already, so let's talk about it. Do you think Jude is telling them to earn God's love? Do you think Jude could be implying their salvation is completely dependent upon them? Provide a passage of Scripture to defend your position.

Look up the following verses and answer the questions. (Note: They are all trick questions.)

EPHESIANS 2:8-9

What did we do to earn salvation? Which works will we be able to boast about that led to our being saved?

ROMANS 9:15-16

How much effort should a person put in to receive God's mercy?

ROMANS 3:23-24

Justification must be pretty expensive. How much can someone pay to get it? How many good works can they do to receive it?

Scripture doesn't contradict itself. When trying to interpret a passage, it's always wise to compare it with other Scriptures so that you can come to a conclusion on the passage most consistent with what Scripture teaches as a whole.

Looking at the passages in Ephesians and Romans, it's pretty clear Jude wasn't saying they must "earn" God's love (as seen in His salvation of them). From the onset, Jude established that they were people who were already loved by God and being kept for God. It is in the sphere of that love that they must put in effort to be kept.

God's sovereignty in salvation ("… kept for Jesus Christ … " [v. 1b]; " … to Him who is able to keep you from stumbling …" [v. 24a]) and man's responsibility ("… keep yourselves in the love of God …" [v. 21a]) are coinciding truths. But keeping yourself in God's love is impossible without already being loved and kept by God.

The apostle Paul communicated this often misunderstood idea in Philippians 2:12 when he said: "Therefore, my beloved, as you have always obeyed, so now, not only as in my presence but much more in my absence, work out your own salvation with fear and trembling …"

If he were to leave it at that, we might've been discouraged, assuming our effort to work out our salvation (not work for our salvation), but what sentence follows? Write it out below.

God's salvation of us and subsequent preservation of us is not going to be without some effort on our part, but lest we think that we're doing it alone or that we will ultimately fail, we need to remind ourselves of whose hand we are being held in (John 10:28-30).

To keep themselves in the love of God, Jude's recipients must do what Jesus said all who abide in His love will do: obey.

The ungodly were obsessively disobedient. They had access to and most likely the doctrinal awareness of God's love. They could've kept themselves in His love if they had the faith to do so, but because they were unwilling to submit to Jesus, they too were unwilling to abide in His love.

We've talked a lot about the sins of the ungodly. By doing the opposite, those who were not "devoid of the Spirit" (v. 19) but being led by the Spirit would continue in God's love. By refusing to submit to the passions, influence, wrong teaching of these ungodly men, they would have inevitably been doing what Jude commanded them to do.

Let's look at some of the sins of the ungodly and determine how we overcome these same temptations in our own lives.

PERVERSION OF GRACE (v. 4)

What would be the godly way to understand God's grace, and how should you live in light of it?

Are you ever tempted to "presume" upon God's grace? If so, how do you resist it?

DENIAL OF JESUS CHRIST (v. 4)

Jesus is both Master and Lord. What would growing in submission to this truth look like for you?

UNBELIEVING (v. 5)

What are some persistent areas of unbelief you've seen in your walk with Christ?

What about God do you need to fight to believe in order to overcome your unbelief?

(For example: Someone might be struggling with sexual sin. There is something about God this person is struggling to believe that has motivated her behavior. She might need to fight to believe that the body is not meant for sexuality immorality but that her body was actually made for the Lord—1 Cor. 6:13.)

SEXUAL IMMORALITY (v. 7)

We all struggle with sexual sin—either practically or mentally. Some women struggle with fornication. Others struggle with what Jude describes as "unnatural desire" (v. 7). Whatever your struggle or area of temptation may be, God wants us to flee sexual immorality (1 Cor. 6:18).

What do you need to do to remain pure in body and mind? (Confess? Repent? Break off certain relationships? Throw away a particular book? Unfollow a specific account?)

REBELLION (vv. 6,8,11)

What command of God do you just not want to obey?

What has God told you to do recently that you've been ignoring?

What fruit do you think God wants to produce in you by your obedience to His Word?

SELFISHNESS/SELF-CENTEREDNESS (v. 12)

What is humility and why should Christians pursue it?

How are you pursuing humility in your own life?

DISCONTENTMENT (v. 16)

Are you content with where God has you and what He's called you to do (namely, to love God and love neighbor)? If not, why? And how can you grow in being content with God's will?

Keeping yourself in the love of God happens naturally as you pursue obedience intentionally. We all have some things we need to grow in. Putting off our old selves (Eph. 4:22) takes time, repentance, faith, effort, tears, confession, prayer, study, and community. But lest we begin to think we will abide in God's love by the strength of our own hands, let us remember this:

If the hearts of the members of the church are right, mockers and scoffers can do very little against them. "Keep yourselves in the love of God"; for a warmhearted company of Christians who love the Lord with all their hearts, and with all their souls, are not likely to be overcome by mockers and sensualists. Love to God will be as a wall of fire round about them. In dull, decaying churches, errors spread like ivy on the crumbling walls of an old abbey, but life, zeal, earnestness, warmheartedness throw off these evils even as a red-hot iron plate evaporates the drops which fall upon it. Love God, and you will not love false doctrine. Keep the heart of the church right, and her head will not go far wrong; let her abide in the love of Jesus, and she will abide in the truth.[2]

CHARLES H. SPURGEON

… he who began a good work in you will bring it to completion at the day of Jesus Christ.

PHILIPPIANS 1:6b

HAVE MERCY

> *And have mercy on those who doubt; save others by snatching them out of the fire; to others show mercy with fear, hating even the garment stained by the flesh.*
>
> **JUDE 22-23**

In the introduction of Jude's Letter, he appealed to his recipients to "contend for the faith" (v. 3). In the body, he showed them why, for which the ungodly people feasting with them are to blame. He began the close of his Letter by instructing the godly on how they should live, and now finally, he was providing instructions on how they should contend.

HAVE MERCY ON THOSE WHO DOUBT

The Greek term for *mercy* being used in verse 22 is *eleéō*—it's translated as to "have pity on" or "have mercy on."[3]

Define:

Pity

_____

_____

_____

_____

Depending on where you got your definition, you most likely saw the word *compassion* being used to define and clarify the word *pity*.

Mercy is simply compassion in action.

Jude mentioned mercy in verse 2. Why?

What does verse 21 say the godly are supposed to do with mercy?

How do you think the prayer to abound in mercy and the instruction to await mercy should shape how you respond to the command to have mercy? Explain.

Who is it that we are to have mercy on?

Notice, Jude made three distinctions on how to be merciful—which tells us that every believer or non-believer might not need the same method even though they all need the same mercy. Practically, it would take wisdom and even some level of depth in the relationship to discern between the three. The doubtful is different from the one who needs to be snatched out of the fire. How you'd contend for the faith in an Ivy League school differs from how you'd contend for the faith with a doubting believer who's a member of a Baptist church in the Bible Belt. I think situations such as these take us back to verse 20 and the need to pray in the Holy Spirit. When we find ourselves wanting to contend in a way that is full of mercy and yet appropriate for the person on whom our mercy is toward, we look to God to guide to us in the way of wisdom (Jas. 1:5.)

Read James 1:6.

How is doubt described?

To doubt is to vacillate—to *go back and forth on what to believe. Is God real? Or is He fake? Is the Bible really authoritative? Or is it a well put together fairy tale? Is Jesus God? Or is He a creation of God?* And there were people, probably Jude's recipients, who were wrestling and unable to land on what was actually true because of the influence of these ungodly men.

Considering the lives and messages of the ungodly teachers, on the topics of Jesus, sin, salvation, or judgment, what might these doubters be struggling to believe?

Every Christian has doubts at some point in their walks. For some, the doubts are seasonal or momentary. For others, the doubts are persistent and lifelong. In those times when doubts are louder than faith, some Christians have taken it upon themselves to be cold, condescending, and judgmental toward those who are doubting. The impatient and less-than-gentle Christian is the Christian who has forgotten mercy.

How should your own experiences with doubt and remembering God's mercy shape how you show mercy to those who are doubting?

Here are some antonyms for mercy (compassion):
- Apathy
- Meanness
- Indifference
- Harshness
- Mercilessness

Let's say a fellow believer in your church confesses to you that she is struggling to believe God will actually judge sin. She grew up believing that to be the case, but now, after reading a book that used several Scriptures to debunk the doctrine of hell, she doesn't really know what she believes.

How do you, as a person who has received mercy and who is awaiting mercy, show mercy to this doubting Christian? (Use the antonyms for compassion as a framework of what not to do and Jude's Letter for what to say).

SAVE OTHERS BY SNATCHING THEM OUT OF THE FIRE

The imagery in Jude's second charge on how to contend for the faith is much different than the first.

> **When you read the words "snatch out of the fire," what comes to your mind about contending for the faith in this way?**

Read the verse below:

> And when the dissension became violent, the tribune, afraid that Paul would be torn to pieces by them, commanded the soldiers to go down and take him away from among them by force and bring him into the barracks.
>
> **ACT 23:10**

Underline the word group that most likely describes the word *snatch*.

> **How does the imagery for snatching in Acts 23:10 help you to understand the phrase "save others by snatching them ..."?**

Before we can understand what it would actually look like to snatch someone out of the fire, we first need to understand what Jude means by fire. After all, the *what* will motivate and inform the *why*.

> **In what context has Jude previously written about fire?**

Let's look at how other New Testament figures used the imagery of fire to understand what Jude is trying to communicate.

- *John the Baptist—Matthew 3:10*

- *Peter—2 Peter 3:7*

- *John—Revelation 20:14-15*

- *Jesus—Matthew 18:8-9*

Comparing all four of these texts, what is the fire in Jude representative of?

Unlike "those who doubt," there was another group of people who were no longer vacillating between truth and falsehood; they had simply begun to believe the lies. There was no longer a wrestle with unbiblical ideas and living, only a gradual submission to sin and false doctrine which they weren't in hell for just yet. But they were playing with fire. Their feet were too close to the flames, and for their safety, they needed to be snatched out.

There is nothing new under the sun. For that reason, today and until the return of Christ, there will be times when our friends, family, church members will not be willing to endure sound doctrine. They'll listen to the teachers teaching what their hearts desire (2 Tim. 4:3). And these teachers are *everywhere*—on social media, in the Christian Living section of the bookstore, in our churches, and so forth. It's not difficult to access these unbiblical messages (Which is why 2 Timothy says that these teachers are *accumulated* because you can't accumulate something that's not already available in abundance.). When this happens to the people close to us, Jude wants us to snatch them, as in contend for the faith forcefully and with urgency.

Snatching someone out of the fire takes intentionality, boldness, biblical clarity, and knowledge. Christians tend to take two kinds of approaches. There is the "all love, no truth" method and the "all truth, no love" method.

Every Christian might find herself on one end of the spectrum at some point. Wherever you may land naturally, answer the questions below:

ALL LOVE, NO TRUTH

Can you think of a time when you shrunk back from sharing a hard biblical truth in the name of "love"?

Can you identify the thoughts, fears, or doubts that kept you from saying the difficult thing?

ALL TRUTH, NO LOVE

Can you think of a time when you were biblically accurate in what you shared but practically loveless in how you shared?

Can you identify the thoughts or prideful perspectives that hindered your love?

In Week 2, we talked about the Christians (and professing Christians) who have taken on the banner of "defenders of the faith" and failed to represent the character of the faithful. When we are tempted to do the same, we have to remember obedience to what God commanded through Jude should be done in submission to the second greatest commandment told to us through Jesus—love our neighbors as ourselves (Matt. 22:36-40).

When tempted to err on the side of timidity, to the point that when we are around people meddling with fire and we don't point out the flames around their feet, be reminded that "God gave us a spirit not of fear but of power and love and self-control" (2 Tim. 1:7).

We can walk in truth and love by simply walking by the Spirit. When a Christian is led by the Spirit in snatching people out of the fire, she can be bold and loving, honest and gentle, faithful and fearless because the Spirit will always lead His own to bear that kind of fruit.

Let's say you find out one of your Christian friends is beginning to identify herself with sins she used to resist because she just doesn't believe a loving God would send people to hell. She wrestled with the doctrine of judgment for a while, she read books and has linked up with other "Christians" who have confirmed that what they used to believe may not be the truth.

How would you snatch her out of the fire?

Romans 11:19-21 shows how you not only experience the fear of God as a right way of worshiping him in reverence and awe, but you experience the fear of God as an incentive not to run away from him. So, it says in Romans 11:19, "You will say, 'Branches were broken off so that I might be grafted in.'" In other words, Jews were rejected so that I, a Gentile, could be grafted into the Abrahamic covenant. Verse 20: "That is true. They were broken off because of their unbelief, but you stand fast through faith. So do not become proud, but fear." So he is commanding believers who are standing fast in faith to fear. Fear what? Fear the prospect of becoming proud, and arrogant, and self-sufficient, and drifting away from the living God in a kind of hard-heartedness. So fear functions as a preservative. We don't want to run away from God.[5]

TO OTHERS SHOW MERCY WITH FEAR, HATING EVEN THE GARMENT STAINED BY THE FLESH

There are others who, being different from the doubtful and possibly in a similar state as those who need to be snatched from the fire, Jude says we are to show mercy to as well. This mercy, or active compassion, is to be shown with fear—the fear of God and, subsequently, His judgment.

How would you explain what it means to "fear God"?

Read the following verses in your Bible:

- *2 Peter 3:11-18*

- *1 Corinthians 10:6-12*

In both verses, what about God is being used as an incentive for the peoples' pursuit of holiness?

John Piper said something key in understanding Jude's use of the word *fear*. He said, "fear functions as a preservative."[4]

Why might Jude be commanding and cautioning his recipients to show mercy with fear (of God and judgment)? What could have happened to them and could happen to us if we don't fear God while trying to display compassion?

With this fear comes hatred. Hatred of what?

> *Now Joshua was standing before the angel, clothed with filthy garments. And the angel said to those who were standing before him, "Remove the filthy garments from him." And to him he said, "Behold, I have taken your iniquity away from you, and I will clothe you with pure vestments.(robes)."*
>
> **ZECHARIAH 3:3-4**

> *Yet you have still a few names in Sardis, people who have not soiled their garments, and they will walk with me in white, for they are worthy.*
>
> **REVELATION 3:4**

> *I said to him, "Sir, you know." And he said to me, "These are the ones coming out of the great tribulation. They have washed their robes and made them white in the blood of the Lamb.*
>
> **REVELATION 7:14**

After reading these verses, what are "garments stained by flesh" (Jude 23) symbolic of (remember what we learned about the flesh in v. 8)?

If we were to summarize Jude verse 23, it would be this:

To others, show _____ , fear _____, and hate _____.

When a well-meaning Christian enters into the ministry of mercy without the fear of God, her compassion can so quickly become complicity and eventually conformity. Showing mercy without fear and hatred of sin makes us all susceptible to fall into the same deceit which has overtaken the one we are ministering to. This is why Jude's instructions in verses 20-21 are so important. Building ourselves up in the faith will anchor us in the truth of God's Word. Praying in the Holy Spirit will increase our dependence upon God and His Spirit. Waiting for God's mercy will keep our eyes on eternity. And all three will keep us in God's love. While there, when walking with a friend living sinfully, we will have the ability to love her well and hate her sin.

We want to be careful to never love others *more than* we love the God who has been merciful to us (Matt. 10:37). Being reverential toward Him in all of our doing will keep our feet away from the fire waiting to swallow us all whole.

Let's say that you have a friend living a sexually immoral life, just like the ungodly in Jude's Letter. How would you show mercy to her, mixed with fear, while hating the sins in which she walks?

> It is a dangerous thing to live for Christ in an atmosphere of false teaching and seductive morals. It is a hazardous thing to try to rescue men for the gospel out of such an environment. If you get too near the fire, it will burn you; if you get too near the garment stained by the flesh, it will defile you. Is withdrawal the answer, then? No. Advance against the forces of evil, face the dangers involved, so long as you are strong in the Lord's might. Such is the thrust, and the context, of Jude's final verses.[6]
>
> **MICHAEL GREEN**

JUDE 24-25

As you watch the Week 6 video, answer the following questions:

- How does Jude begin and end his Letter?
- Who came without blemish to die so that all who believe would be cleansed of their sins?
- Who do we submit to? Who is the only one with ultimate authority over our lives?
- How did God use His power and dominion?

After watching the Week 6 video, discuss the following together as a group:

- What are you a slave to?
- We are not alone as we contend for the faith. How can you help each other contend?
- How do you give glory to God at school, at home, at practice, and at work?
- List four words you would use to describe God.

> NOW TO HIM WHO IS ABLE TO KEEP YOU FROM STUMBLING AND TO PRESENT YOU BLAMELESS BEFORE THE PRESENCE OF HIS GLORY WITH GREAT JOY, ²⁵TO THE ONLY GOD, OUR SAVIOR, THROUGH JESUS CHRIST OUR LORD, BE GLORY, MAJESTY, DOMINION, AND AUTHORITY, BEFORE ALL TIME AND NOW AND FOREVER. AMEN.
>
> JUDE 24-25

Jude began his Letter with a prayer to God (v. 2). Now Jude is closing his Letter with praise to God. This doxology has been a favorite of Christians for centuries, probably because of how hopeful it is. Imagine how Jude's recipients might've felt while hearing Jude's Letter, so much of it being about the ungodly, judgment, and false teaching. Then the closing with instructions on how to contend for the faith, which included the command to fear God and His judgment lest they fall like those around them. By this point, this doxology would've been their "exhale," their chance to respond in praise for who God is, what He's done, and what He will do.

NOW TO HIM

> Now to him who is able to keep you from stumbling and to present you blameless before the presence of his glory with great joy,
>
> **JUDE 24-25**

In the same way that Jude's greeting follows the basic format of name of sender, name of recipient, and words of blessing/thanksgiving, doxologies have their own structure. Doxologies always include: Addressee, Honor, Duration, Response.[1]

Let's look at a doxology written by Paul found at the end of his Letter to the Romans.

> Now to him who is able to strengthen you according to my gospel and the preaching of Jesus Christ, according to the revelation of the mystery that was kept secret for long ages but has now been disclosed and through the prophetic writings has been made known to all nations, according to the command of the eternal God, to bring about the obedience of faith—to the only wise God be glory forevermore through Jesus Christ! Amen.
>
> **ROMANS 16:25-27**

ADDRESSEE: "Now to him who is able to strengthen you according to my gospel and the preaching of Jesus Christ, according to the revelation of the mystery that was kept secret for long ages but has now been disclosed and through the prophetic writings has been made known to all nations, according to the command of the eternal God, to bring about the obedience of faith ..." (Rom. 16:25-26).

HONOR: "... to the only wise God be glory ..." (Rom. 16:27a).

DURATION: "... be glory forevermore through Jesus Christ!" (Rom. 16:27b)

RESPONSE: "Amen" (Rom. 16:27b).

> **DOXOLOGY:** From the Greek word Doxa meaning "glory, splendor, grandeur" + the Greek word Logos meaning "word or speaking" = Words of praise to God[2]

Looking at Jude's doxology, let's identify these same components.

1. Underline the addressee.

2. Put brackets around the honor.

3. Circle the duration.

4. Put two lines underneath the response.

> *Now to him who is able to keep you from stumbling and to present you blameless before the presence of his glory with great joy, to the only God, our Savior, through Jesus Christ our Lord, be glory, majesty, dominion, and authority, before all time and now and forever. Amen.*

Over the course of this week, we will be studying each component of Jude's doxology. Let's begin with the addressee.

NOW TO HIM WHO IS ABLE TO KEEP YOU FROM STUMBLING AND TO PRESENT YOU BLAMELESS BEFORE THE PRESENCE OF HIS GLORY WITH GREAT JOY

In Jude's greeting, he said something similar to this? What was it?

If we were to take that as is (without any consideration of the context or any study of the biblical understanding of God's preservation of His church) we would've only known who they (and we) were being kept for (Jesus Christ). But we wouldn't have known who was doing the keeping.

In Jude's doxology, before we learn the name of "Him" who is keeping us, we learn how He is keeping us. What word, in the beginning of verse 24, points to God's power (hint, hint) to keep His own? Circle it.

Here are three other New Testament texts that use the same word. In each verse, underline what God is able to do.

> And do not presume to say to yourselves, "We have Abraham as our father," for I tell you, God is able from these stones to raise up children for Abraham.
>
> **MATTHEW 3:9**

> And as Jesus passed on from there, two blind men followed him, crying aloud, "Have mercy on us, Son of David." When he entered the house, the blind men came to him, and Jesus said to them, "Do you believe that I am able to do this?" They said to him, "Yes, Lord." Then he touched their eyes, saying, "According to your faith be it done to you." And their eyes were opened.
>
> **MATTHEW 9:27-30a**

> Don't fear those who kill the body but are not able to kill the soul; rather, fear him who is able to destroy both soul and body in hell.
>
> **MATTHEW 10:28 (CSB)**

Notice that in these verses in particular, God is able to do what humans are unable to do, i.e. destroy both body and soul in hell; heal blindness; make children for Abraham out of stones. God has the power to do what we would never be able to do on our own, which is to keep us from stumbling.

The language of "falling" or "stumbling" is so commonly used to describe our occasional moral indiscretions that we can easily read how it's used in verse 24 as "to Him who is able to keep you from [falling into sin today]." But this would be the wrong way to understand what Jude means by "stumbling".

We know that even as people who have been empowered to say no to the flesh (Rom. 8:12-13), the flesh still has passions that wage war against our souls (1 Pet. 2:11), which we all will at times fail at resisting. When we repent of giving into temptation, God will forgive and cleanse us (1 John 1:9). So Jude's emphasis here was not on God keeping us from sin (which He can and does through His Spirit), but he was more so highlighting the final preservation of those who have been called, loved, and thus, kept. This "stumbling" is eschatological in nature in that he spoke of them being kept in God's love, never failing to obtain His mercy on the day of judgment (v. 21). He was praising God for the fact that even though the godly might be tested, tempted, and at times, trip, because God is powerful enough to do it, He will be faithful to keep them from falling forever.

Read the following verses to see how other New Testament writers spoke about this same praiseworthy reality:

- *Romans 8:30*
- *1 Corinthians 1:8*
- *Philippians 1:6*

Read Psalm 121. The psalmist reiterates the same praise in the Old Testament.

Jude praises God for being able to keep the godly, and in the latter portion of verse 24 he acknowledges that God will also present the godly before Himself as blameless. (Small note: In the Greek, the word translated *present* also means *stand*.[3] Jude was giving us a beautiful image with his words about a God who will keep us from falling and stand us before Him as blameless.)

The Greek word translated *blameless* literally means "without blemish."[4]

> *If you can recall, Jude has been explicitly and implicitly using the Old Testament throughout his Letter. What Old Testament ordinance is he making reference to with the words "without blemish"? Look up Leviticus 1:1-4 and Deuteronomy 17:1 to help form your answer.*

> *What did God demand of Israel's sacrifices (offerings)?*

The holy and eternally sinless God also demanded the same of His creation.

Read Psalm 15 in your Bible and then Psalm 24:3-4 below.

> *Who shall ascend the hill of the Lord? And who shall stand in his holy place? He who has clean hands and a pure heart, who does not lift up his soul to what is false and does not swear deceitfully.*
> **PSALM 24:3-4**

What kind of person can stand in the presence of God?

Seeing that Jude's recipients were a people who need and had received mercy (vv. 3,22), what would that tell you about what they must've deserved instead of mercy, in stark contrast to what Jude says they'd be presented as?

To be blameless is to be without fault. Scripture says that "all have sinned and fall short of the glory of God" (Rom. 6:23). It also says that "no one does good, not even one" (Rom. 3:12b). So how in the world would Jude's recipients, and how would we, be presented before God as blameless when we've sinned our entire lives? (*Rhetorical question*)

> *For if the blood of goats and bulls, and the sprinkling of defiled persons with the ashes of a heifer, sanctify for the purification of the flesh, how much more will the blood of Christ, who through the eternal Spirit offered himself without blemish to God, purify our conscience from dead works to serve the living God.*
> **HEBREWS 9:13-14**

Who has no blemishes (no sin)?

> *And you, who once were alienated and hostile in mind, doing evil deeds, he has now reconciled in his body of flesh by his death, in order to present you holy and blameless and above reproach before him.*
> **COLOSSIANS 1:21-22**

What did the sinless one have to do to present you blameless?

It is on the basis of Christ's blamelessness and Christ's sacrificial death (as the perfect spotless Lamb) that all who are in Christ will be presented before God blameless just like Christ (Rom. 8:1).

Where does Jude say this presentation will take place?

Read the following verses and answer the corresponding question.
- *Isaiah 6:1-5*
- *Ezekiel 1:28*
- *Revelation 1:17-18*

What usually accompanies the experience of being in God's presence, and how do these descriptions help you to understand the gravity of one day being in His presence without fault?

The godly will one day stand in the presence of God, a presence that is terrifying and holy (Heb 12:21). The ungodly Jude spoke about would not be able to stand triumphantly or with confidence in His presence. They would want to hide from the destruction Jude said has been designated for them (v. 4). Before God, they would meet all of the wrath they had stored up. But for the godly, they would be presented blameless with great joy. There, the Judge would also be their Savior, Redeemer, Brother, Friend.

Read Isaiah 25:8-9 and Revelation 19:6-8 in your Bible. How do both texts relate to Jude 24, specifically regarding what the godly will do in God's presence.

Thinking about all you learned about God from Jude, especially considering all that the gospel has provided for you, what do you think you'd rejoice about while standing in His presence?

> *God shall arise, his enemies shall be scattered; and those who hate him shall flee before him! As smoke is driven away, so you shall drive them away; as wax melts before fire, so the wicked shall perish before God! But the righteous shall be glad; they shall exult before God; they shall be jubilant with joy!*
> **PSALM 68:1-3**

DAY 2

TO THE ONLY GOD

> *"To the only God, our Savior, through Jesus Christ our Lord ..."*
> **JUDE 25**

TO THE ONLY GOD

In your own words, what is idolatry?

Which commandment(s) (as given by God to Moses in Exodus 20) address idolatry? Write them below.

Read Isaiah 44:6-20.

In verse 8, God says,"Is there a God besides me?" In verses 9-20, we are given a description of someone making an idol. In verse 17, how is the idol referred to? How does verse 8 show us the deception and foolishness of what is said in verse 17?

Is every idol something that is made? Why or why not?

> Not only are the readers presented blameless or without fault, but also "with great joy." This joy is not a private joy ("I am so happy"), although certainly that is what would be felt, but a public joy ("We rejoice before him"). The great joy refers to an eschatological celebration, the appropriate festivity when God delivers his people.[5]
>
> **PETER H. DAVIDS**

Read Romans 1:24-25.

In idolatry, who and what is exchanged? What is worshiped and served instead?

Idolatry is so terrible because it's the act of honoring (worshiping) what God has made and treating it like it's Him. The idol worshiper expects of the idol what only God can ultimately and eternally provide. The man in Isaiah 44 makes an idol with wood, using one half to warm himself and praying to the other half for deliverance (v. 15). Clearly, wood is useful for many things, as God created it to be, but deliverance is not one. Only the true and living God can deliver us.

Read Colossians 3:5 below:

> *Put to death therefore what is earthly in you: sexual immorality, impurity, passion, evil desire, and covetousness, which is idolatry.*

Idolatry doesn't only describe a person physically bowing down to an actual object. It also includes the desires of the heart that motivate our behavior. We see in the verse above covetousness is called idolatry. Covetous people are those who desire what does not belong to them. They haven't actively bowed down to anything with their bodies, but Paul is saying that their hearts are worshiping what they don't have in exchange for the worship of God. God being God. God being all satisfying. God being more than enough. Their discontentment is because they've believed a lie (Rom. 1:24-25), primarily the lie that what they want is greater than who they should want.

Read over Jude's letter.

> *Write down the verses that would correspond to some of the idols of the ungodly:*
>
> *1. Serving Self*
>
> *2. Physical Pleasure/Sex*
>
> *3. Money/Power/Esteem*

In Paul's letter to the Galatians, he said, "Formerly, when you did not know God, you were enslaved to those that by nature are not gods" (Gal. 4:8). Though Paul was talking to the church in Galatia, this verse is also true of us. Before knowing God, we were all slaves to people and things that weren't worthy of our worship.

> *On the following page, list some of the idols you were enslaved to. Below each, write down the lies you believed about the idols. (What did you think this false god could give you that you didn't trust the true God to provide?) Finally, write down the truth about God that you've come to believe.*

For example:

- **Idol:** *Relationships*

- **Lie:** *I thought I needed a romantic relationship, no matter how immoral it might've been, to give me the comfort I so desperately wanted.*

- **Truth:** *God is the source of all comfort, not people (2 Cor. 1:3).*

- *Idol:*

- *Lie:*

- *Truth:*

- *Idol:*

- *Lie:*

- *Truth:*

- *Idol:*

- *Lie:*

- *Truth:*

Now, coming back to Jude's praise, "to the only God," what is this praise in opposition to?

Remembering what you yourself have been set free from, how should this praise affect you?

For they themselves report concerning us the kind of reception we had among you, and how you turned to God from idols to serve the living and true God, and to wait for his Son from heaven, whom he raised from the dead, Jesus who delivers us from the wrath to come.

1 THESSALONIANS 1:9-10

OUR SAVIOR

Do you find it odd that God, referring to God the Father, is also being called Savior in this verse?

Look at the chart below and note which way the author addresses God— as Father or as Son—in each verse.

VERSE	FATHER OR SON
Acts 5:31-32	
Acts 13:23	
1 Timothy 1:1	
1 Timothy 4:10	
Titus 1:4	
Titus 3:4-6	

It's not a contradiction for both God the Father and Jesus to be referred to as Savior. It reveals the unity of the Godhead in accomplishing the task of salvation.

Read John 3:16. Because of God the Father's love for the world, who did God send into the world?

Read John 6:38-40. What was the will of the Father and what part did Jesus have to play in this will being done?

Read 1 John 4:14. Why did God send His Son into the world?

In Jude 3, Jude said salvation is something they all share. How did God the Father and His Son Jesus Christ work together in making this salvation available to all?

So now, in your own words, explain why Jude would call God the Father, their Savior:

THROUGH JESUS CHRIST OUR LORD

Let's take a look at all the great things God has done for us through His Son, Jesus Christ.

FORGIVEN US

> *Of Him all the prophets bear witness that through His name everyone who believes in Him receives forgiveness of sins.*
>
> **ACTS 10:43, NASB**

MADE US CONQUERORS

No, in all these things we are more than conquerors through him who loved us.

ROMANS 8:37

GIVEN US ACCESS TO THE FATHER

For through him we both have access in one Spirit to the Father.

EPHESIANS 2:18

STRENGTHENED US

I can do all things through him who strengthens me.

PHILIPPIANS 4:13

TAUGHT US TO PRAISE

Through him then let us continually offer up a sacrifice of praise to God, that is, the fruit of lips that acknowledge his name.

HEBREWS 13:15

GIVEN US LIFE

In this the love of God was made manifest among us, that God sent his only Son into the world, so that we might live through him.

1 JOHN 4:9

GIVEN US VICTORY

But thanks be to God, who gives us the victory through our Lord Jesus Christ.

1 CORINTHIANS 15:57

PROVIDED COMFORT

For as we share abundantly in Christ's sufferings, so through Christ we share abundantly in comfort too.

2 CORINTHIANS 1:5

MADE US ABLE TO OFFER ACCEPTABLE SACRIFICES

> *You yourselves like living stones are being built up as a spiritual house, to be a holy priesthood, to offer spiritual sacrifices acceptable to God through Jesus Christ.*
> **1 PETER 2:5**

MADE US ABLE TO DRAW NEAR TO GOD

> *Consequently, he is able to save to the uttermost those who draw near to God through him, since he always lives to make intercession for them.*
> **HEBREWS 7:25**

GIVEN US SALVATION

> *For God did not send his Son into the world to condemn the world, but in order that the world might be saved through him.*
> **JOHN 3:17**

Thank God for Jesus—for it is through Him we have received many, many, many good things!

PRAISE BREAK

> *Blessed be the LORD, the God of Israel, who alone does wondrous things. Blessed be his glorious name forever; may the whole earth be filled with his glory! Amen and Amen!*
> **PSALM 72:18-19**

Remembering what we learned about the continuity between God the Father and God the Son in the work of salvation, what might Jude have meant when he said, "to the only God, our Savior, through Christ Jesus our Lord" (v. 24)?

How many times has Jesus been referred to as Lord in Jude's epistle?

The fruit of being mastered by the flesh is evident in all that is described of the ungodly. How would their descriptions change if they no longer denied Jesus as Master and Lord and, instead, submitted to Him? (Use Gal. 5:16-26 and Col. 3:5-17 as reference points. I've answered the first couple for you.)

- **Slave to sin:** Perverting the grace of God as license to sin (v. 4)

- **Slave to God:** Contend for the faith (v. 3)

- **Slave to sin:** Defile the flesh (v. 8)

- **Slave to God:** Not gratifying the desires of the flesh; putting to death what is earthly (Gal. 5:16; Col. 3:5)

- **Slave to sin:** Reject authority (v. 8)

- **Slave to God:**

- **Slave to sin:** Blaspheme the glorious ones (v. 8)

- **Slave to God:**

- **Slave to sin:** Shepherds feeding themselves (v. 12)

- **Slave to God:**

- **Slave to sin:** Malcontent (v. 16)

- **Slave to God:**

- **Slave to sin:** Scoffer (v. 18)

- **Slave to God:**

- **Slave to sin:** Divisive (v. 19)

- **Slave to God:**

Unlike the ungodly, the godly submit to Jesus Christ as Master and Lord. Considering this was not always the case, that we all once lived submitted to things that weren't God and therefore not eligible to be our Lord, how did God's salvation help you submit to the right Master (Rom. 6:22)?

How is God's grace continually teaching you how to grow in your submission to our Master, Jesus Christ (Titus 2:11-12)?

DAY 3

BE GLORY

Be glory, majesty, dominion, and authority
JUDE 25

GLORY

What comes to your mind when you think of the word glory?

God's glory is a pretty complex and therefore difficult concept to explain. Perhaps because God is understandable and mysterious all at the same time. Most likely because we are inherently unlike Him (Isa. 55:8). We were created for His glory and we are, through Jesus Christ, able to give Him glory because He is glorious.

Read Exodus 33:17-33; 34:1-9.

What are some of the attributes and actions that would be considered "God's glory"?

Why do you think God told Moses he wouldn't be able to see His glory? How does it make Jude 24 even more incredible?

If you enjoy a good hymn every now and again, like me, then these lyrics will be quite familiar to you:

Why do you think the hymn writer described Jesus as a "cleft"?

What has God, our Savior, through Jesus Christ our Lord, done for us so that we can see Him with great joy (in contrast to great fear and death)?

Beloved, we are God's children now, and what we will be has not yet appeared; but we know that when he appears we shall be like him, because we shall see him as he is.
1 JOHN 3:2

God's glory was made manifest to all through His Son. But know this, God's glory was (and still is) intrinsic to who He was (and is) even before it was seen in what God has done (and will do).

> *And the Word became flesh and dwelt among us, and we have seen his glory, glory as of the only Son from the Father, full of grace and truth. (John bore witness about him, and cried out, "This was he of whom I said, 'He who comes after me ranks before me, because he was before me.'") For from his fullness we have all received, grace upon grace. For the law was given through Moses; grace and truth came through Jesus Christ. No one has ever seen God; the only God, who is at the Father's side, he has made him known.*

JOHN 1:14-18

So God deserves glory because He is eternally glorious. It is through this glory that we have all received what Moses was unable to see with his own eyes. Through Christ we've received the grace and mercy He passed by Moses with. God told Moses "I will be gracious to whom I will be gracious, and will show mercy on whom I will show mercy" (Ex. 33:19b). And He has done just that for us.

It's because of this glorious God and to this glorious God all saints should and can join in praise with Jude by saying "to the only God, … be glory!" (v. 25).

MAJESTY

Greek: *megalósuné*
Root: *Megas—Pronounced 'Meg-as'*[7]

Guess which English word comes from the Greek word megas.

Define:

Mega
_____
_____
_____
_____

Read 1 Chronicles 29:10-16.

As David prays to the Lord, he ascribed to Him five things, one of which is "majesty" (v. 11). What did David praise God for that could be attributed to His being majestic/great? List them all below. (I filled in the first and last one for you, now you do the rest.)

1. Yours is the kingdom, O LORD

2.

3.

4.

5.

6.

7.

8.

9. O LORD our God, all this abundance that we have provided ... comes from your hand and is all your own

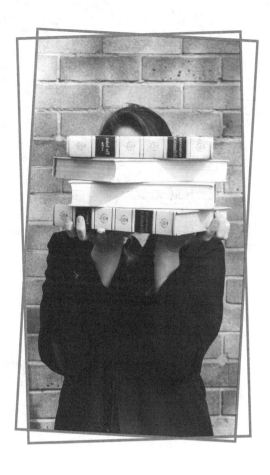

The greatness of God speaks to His absolute rule over all things. His endless resources. His unimaginable power to do as He pleases and for whomever He pleases. He is King of all, even of those who would deny (v. 4) the One who upholds the universe with word of His power (Heb 1:3).

When people enter into the presence of a royal, who has but a fraction of the majesty that God has, they are expected to bow out of honor. The majestic one whom they stand in front of inspires awe and reverence. But this God, our Savior, is the true King and the only God. He dwells in unapproachable light (1 Tim. 6:16). He sits on a throne, surrounded by creatures that live to give Him glory. We haven't even scratched the surface of understanding the majestic nature of God. But with the little knowledge we do have, we join Jude's praise by saying, "to the only God ... be majesty" (v. 25)!

DOMINION AND AUTHORITY

To say God has dominion is to say God has power.

Read Isaiah 40:9-26 in your Bible.

How would you take what Isaiah said about God and use it to explain His might or power? (Use the specific examples from the Isaiah passage but rephrase them in your own words.)

Read Luke 1:46-55 in your Bible.

How would you take what Mary said about God and use it to explain His might or power? (Use the specific examples from the passage in Luke.)

God not only has dominion but He also has the authority to exercise it. His authority to do a particular thing is in partnership with His ability (power) to do it.

Read each passage below and write down what God has the dominion and authority to do. I've done the first one for you.

	JESUS HAS THE AUTHORITY AND POWER TO:
Matthew 9:1-8	*Forgive sins*
Luke 12:4-5	
John 10:17-18	
John 17:1-2	
Romans 13:1	

The God Jude is praising is one who has the dominion and right to do whatever He pleases. And unlike many of the men and women who have received a measure of authority and power and used it to serve themselves, such as presidents, kings, bosses, parents, CEOs, police officers, church pastors, and leaders (Jude 12), God has continually used His power and authority to serve others (Matt. 20:28).

> Have this mind among yourselves, which is yours in Christ Jesus, who, though he was in the form of God, did not count equality with God a thing to be grasped, but emptied himself, by taking the form of a servant, being born in the likeness of men. And being found in human form, he humbled himself by becoming obedient to the point of death, even death on a cross.
>
> **PHILIPPIANS 2:5-8**

It is this God, through Christ Jesus, by whose dominion and authority we have been given the right to be called children of God (John 1:12), that we praise with Jude, by saying "to the only God … be dominion and authority (v. 25)!"

BEFORE ALL TIME AND NOW AND FOREVER

Choose at least two of the passages below to look up in your own Bible. How do these texts help you to understand the duration of God's attributes (glory, majesty, dominion, and authority) and what that should mean for how long He is worthy of praise?

- *Malachi 3:6*

- *Romans 11:36*

- *Galatians 1:3-5*

- *Philippians 4:20*

- *2 Timothy 4:18*

- *Hebrews 13:8*

While contending for the faith in a world that might not look like it's in subjection to God (Heb. 2:8) …

When trying to keep yourself from the lie that what God has made is more glorious than Him …

When being tempted to bow down to lesser kings …

When wondering if God is still in control and if He still has the power to keep the godly and judge the ungodly …

When trying to remain anchored to the faith that describes God as being full of glory, the King of kings, with all power and authority in His hand, while at the same time defending these same truths to others who are denying Him …

… how should the eternal nature of God's character encourage and challenge you?

DAY 4

AMEN

> *To the only God, our Savior, through Jesus Christ our Lord, be glory, majesty, dominion, and authority, before all time and now and forever. Amen.*
> **JUDE 25**

Amen is used regularly by Christians during and after fellowship, prayer, worship, and the preaching of God's Word. Most of us have a sense of what we are intending to communicate by saying *amen*, and some of us don't. But this word holds weight, much of which is lost on us. Maybe because of the frequency with which we say it or because we haven't studied its use in the Scriptures which would provide theological depth to a seemingly common word. So let's take some time to learn about it from God's Word so that we can understand what Jude is expecting of all who would read his letter, then and now.

Read Deuteronomy 27:15-19 in your Bible. If all of the people were to say "amen" after hearing all of the judgments that awaited the wicked, what would their response have signified?

> Amen: Hebrew word meaning "so it is" or "let it be," derived from a verb meaning "to be firm or sure." Some translations of the Bible always retain the Hebrew word *amen* in the text. Others translate it by an expression such as "truly" or "I tell you the truth … "[8]
>
> **WALTER A. ELWELL AND PHILIP WESLEY COMFORT**

We are used to hearing *amen* proclaimed after a blessing has been spoken, but rarely—well, at least in my context—do we hear it as a response to curses. It might seem unloving or "intolerant" for God's people to say *amen* to the pronouncement of judgment on the wicked. Similar to this portion of Deuteronomy, Jude's letter spoke about the judgment awaiting the ungodly as well.

If after these curses were pronounced and God's people refused to say *amen* in response, they in essence would be saying, "We don't agree with what has been said. And we don't affirm it as true."

That being the case, why is it a good thing for them to say amen?

When what has been spoken is biblical and therefore true, whether in preaching, prayer, worship, and so on, our amens should be informed by our faith and not merely by our opinions.

With what we learned during Weeks 3 and 4 about the holiness of God, what must we believe to be true about Him to help us say yes and amen to the difficult things Jude has written?

To say amen in response to the pronouncement of judgment is not an act of rejoicing. We don't delight in the reality that God will execute judgment on the ungodly (Jude 15). We do trust that because God is good (Ps. 119:68) and wise (Rom. 11:33) and His judgments are just (Rev. 19:2a), to say amen is simply to affirm that what He's said (through His Word) will happen. To disagree with His Word is ultimately to disagree with Him.

> *Jesus answered him, "Truly, truly, I say to you, unless one is born again he cannot see the kingdom of God."*
> **JOHN 3:3**

Circle the word that Jesus uses twice in the passage above.

In Greek, this word is *amēn*, with its origins in Hebrew.[9]

In the verse below, write the Greek in place of the English repeated word.

> *Jesus answered him, "_____, _____, I say to you, unless one is born again he cannot see the kingdom of God."*

The use of *amen* in response to curses for the people of God would be a "so it is" and "let it be" (from the previous definition). Jesus is using it differently in that here it isn't in response to something spoken but it precedes what He speaks.

What is Jesus trying to convey by saying amēn amēn?

Jesus spoke with authoritative certainty. What follows "Truly, truly" or "Amen, amen" should be taken with the seriousness and faith that they deserve. In other words, Jesus is essentially saying, "What I am about to say is entirely true and important, so listen."

Read Psalm 41:13, 72:19, 89:52, and 106:48.

Quick Test: Is the structure of these four Psalms benedictional or doxological?

The psalmist blesses the Lord and closes each psalm with "Amen and Amen." Why do you think he added the amens? What was he communicating by ending his exaltation of God with those two words? (Feel free to refer to the definition on page 159.)

Coming back around to Jude's doxology:

> *Now to him who is able to keep you from stumbling and to present you blameless before the presence of his glory with great joy, to the only God, our Savior, through Jesus Christ our Lord, be glory, majesty, dominion, and authority, before all time and now and forever. Amen.*

JUDE 24-25

Let's take it apart so we can really gather what it is that Jude wants us to say *amen* to.

NOW TO HIM WHO IS WHO ABLE TO KEEP YOU FROM STUMBLING

How does your amen affirm the truth of this statement?

NOW TO HIM WHO IS ABLE ... TO PRESENT YOU BLAMELESS BEFORE THE PRESENCE OF HIS GLORY WITH GREAT JOY

What does your amen say about the reality of this statement?

TO THE ONLY GOD, OUR SAVIOR

What happened that allowed you to say amen to this and mean it?

THROUGH CHRIST JESUS OUR LORD

Who in Jude's letter can't say amen to this? (If by their lives, they didn't live like He's Lord, then their amen was insincere.)

TO THE ONLY GOD ... BE GLORY

Does this deserve an amen? Why?

TO THE ONLY GOD ... BE MAJESTY

Or this? Why?

TO THE ONLY GOD ... BE DOMINION AND AUTHORITY

In our current cultural climate, which of Jude's instructions will help you continue to say amen to this?

NOW AND FOREVER

What does saying amen to this do for your hope (v. 21)?

The last word of Jude's doxology is so much more than a popular way to close. With *amen* he pointed to what God will do (v. 24) and who God is (v. 25), and he is beckoning all the saints who have been called by this glorious God, loved by this majestic God, and kept by this authoritative God to express the truthfulness of His words with an *amen*. They were certain what he'd said would happen. They were in full agreement in their hearts and with their mouths that God is all of the above and more.

The same cannot be said of the ungodly in Jude's letter. They have denied God; but as for the godly, they believed Him. All the promises of God are yes (*amen*) in Jesus Christ (2 Cor. 1:20), so there is even more assurance that God will keep His word to them. They are in Him. They have been brought near to God through Him. And they are being kept by Him. What better way for Jude to end his letter than in praise.

Praise to the only God, our Savior, through Jesus Christ our Lord. To Him, be glory, majesty, dominion and authority, before time all time and now and forever.

And all of God's people say _____!

DAY 5

WRITE YOUR OWN DOXOLOGY

At the beginning of each week we prayed for God to show us Himself in Jude's letter. At the end of each week, we wrote down what it was that we learned about God. Now, following in the tradition of Jude, Paul, Peter, King David, and others, we will write out our own doxology, which is our own written praise to God. Surely learning and digging into God's holiness and how it's expressed in God's hatred of sin should've made us thankful for God's mercy toward us. As we show mercy to those who doubt, resting in the power (dominion) of God that Jude told us about, we should be inclined to praise Him for His strength. The strength that comes from God is what's keeping us strong and helping us to keep ourselves in His love. Seeing God as He is should lead us to worship God for who He is.

You're going to write your own doxology using the standard structure:

- **Addressee**
- **Honor**
- **Duration**
- **Response**

It can be as long or as short as you want.

The following passages are four examples of New Testament doxologies. Try to avoid copying them. Use them as a point of reference for how to praise God in your own words. This isn't Jude's worship; it's yours.

> *Now to him who is able to do far more abundantly than all that we ask or think, according to the power at work within us, to him be glory in the church and in Christ Jesus throughout all generations, forever and ever. Amen.*
> **EPHESIANS 3:20-21**

> *To the King of ages, immortal, invisible, the only God, be honor and glory forever and ever. Amen.*
> **1 TIMOTHY 1:17**

> *He who is the blessed and only Sovereign, the King of kings and Lord of lords, who alone has immortality, who dwells in unapproachable light, whom no one has ever seen or can see. To him be honor and eternal dominion. Amen.*
> **1 TIMOTHY 6:15b-16**

> *To him who loves us and has freed us from our sins by his blood and made us a kingdom, priests to his God and Father, to him be glory and dominion forever and ever. Amen.*
> **REVELATION 1:5b-6**

YOUR DOXOLOGY

CLOSING

As you watch the Week 7 video, answer the following questions:

- How has your perspective of the Book of Jude changed since the beginning of this study?
- What are the main themes from the Book of Jude?
- What Old Testament stories stood out to you from this study that you were reminded of?
- How is the theme of mercy reiterated and why is this so important?

After watching the Week 7 video, discuss the following together as a group:

- What stood out to you in the video teaching?
- Do you have any unanswered questions about the Book of Jude?
- How are we to contend for the faith every day and point others back to God?
- Who has God called you to share your faith with and show compassion and empathy to?

_____

_____

_____

_____

_____

_____

_____

_____

LEADER GUIDE

A WORD TO THE LEADER

Thanks for taking on the responsibility of leading this group of teen girls! I hope you will be encouraged and challenged as you lead this study. Below, find some tips to help you effectively lead the group study times:

GROUP SESSIONS

Each group session contains the following elements:

GATHER: This is a time to greet and welcome everyone and then to get them talking. In the first session, I've provided some icebreaker questions. In the following sessions, you'll notice a list of questions to help participants review the previous week's personal study. Feel free to adapt, skip, or add questions according to the needs of your group.

WATCH: Each week you'll show a teaching video. Encourage girls to take notes on the Watch pages in their Bible study books.

DISCUSS: During this time, you'll help your group debrief what they heard on the video teaching. A couple of discussion questions are provided on each session's Watch page. Again, feel free to adapt, skip, or add questions as needed to encourage discussion.

PERSONAL STUDY

Each session contains four days of personal study to help girls dig into God's Word for themselves. Week 6 provides an additional activity for a fifth day of study to reflect on and put into practice what girls have learned from the Book of Jude.

PREPARE

STUDY: Watch the teaching video and complete each week's personal study before the group session. Review the discussion questions and consider how best to lead your group through this time.

PRAY: Set aside time each week to pray for yourself and each member of your group.

CONNECT: Find ways to interact and stay engaged with each girl in your group throughout the study. Make use of social media, email, texts, and handwritten notes to encourage them. Continue these connections even after the study ends.

WEEK 1

GATHER

Welcome everyone to the study and distribute a Bible study book to each participant. Encourage girls to get to know one another with a few icebreaker activities.

- Ask everyone to share their name, grade, and favorite candy.

- Consider playing a round of two truths and a lie to better get to know your group.

- Play Candy Q&A by passing out colored candy to each girl and asking specific questions based on the color of the candy. For example, ask each girl holding a blue candy if she has any pets.

Read Jude aloud as a group, perhaps taking turns reading, before watching the video.

WATCH

Watch the Week 1 video as a group. Answer the first set of questions on the Week 1 Watch page (p. 11).

DISCUSS

After watching the video, discuss the second set of questions.

Pray together that the time you spend studying God's Word will lead you to grow not only in your knowledge of God, but in your love for Him, as well.

Remind everyone to do the personal study pages (pp. 12-31) this week, encouraging girls to jot down questions they may have to discuss with the group next week.

_____

_____

_____

_____

_____

_____

WEEK 2

GATHER

Welcome everyone back to the study. Invite girls to ask questions they had from their personal study during the week. Encourage further discussion with the following questions:

- What did you learn this past week about Jude, the brother of Jesus, that you didn't know before?

- The recipients of Jude's letter had been effectually called by God, and they were also loved by God. Do you think God's love motivated God's call? Explain by using Scripture(s) to defend your position.

- Remember what we learned about God and Jude's recipients in our last session? What kind of people were they? How did their description contrast with who God is?

- What did you learn about God or yourself this week through studying Jude?

WATCH
Watch the Week 2 video as a group. Answer the first set of questions on the Week 2 Watch page (p. 33).

DISCUSS
After watching the video, discuss the remaining questions.

Pray together, praising God for your calling and His love and mercy.

Remind everyone to do the personal study pages (pp. 34-59) this week, encouraging girls to jot down questions they may have to discuss with the group next week.

_____

_____

_____

_____

_____

WEEK 3

GATHER
Welcome everyone back to the study. Invite girls to ask questions they had from their personal study during the week.

Encourage further discussion with the following questions:

- Why do you think salvation is a running theme throughout Jude's letter (p. 37)?

- What's going on in his readers' lives that compelled Jude to write this letter? How do you usually discern what's necessary to say (p. 40)?

- Thinking through what it would look like to struggle with others in defense of God's Word and the explicit teachings in Scripture that our culture fights tooth and nail to defy, what does Jude's use of the word _agónízomai_ (contend) do for your understanding of how you should approach contending for the faith?

- Looking at the essentials of the faith on pages 54-57, which five essentials of the faith listed do you feel well-equipped to contend for? Which five essentials of the faith do you feel ill-equipped to contend for? In your own cultural context, what essentials of the faith do you find yourself having to address consistently?

WATCH
Watch the Week 3 video as a group. Answer the first set of questions on the Week 3 Watch page (p. 61).

DISCUSS
After watching the video, discuss the remaining questions.

Pray together that you might grow in understanding of the essentials of the faith and that you would have boldness and discernment as you contend for the faith.

Remind everyone to do the personal study pages (pp. 62-81) this week, encouraging them to jot down questions they may have to discuss with the group next week.

_____

_____

_____

_____

_____

_____

WEEK 4

GATHER

Welcome everyone back to the study. Invite girls to ask questions they had from their personal study during the week. Encourage further discussion with the following questions:

- God delivered Israel from Egypt in a miraculous and mighty act. Many (really thousands) of the same people who were saved from Egypt were destroyed in the wilderness. What do you think Jude wanted his recipients to understand by using this particular example (p. 66)?

- Jude said the judgment of Sodom and Gomorrah serves as an example for us. How? Why do you think we need this as an example (p. 70)?

- This week of personal study featured many stories from the Old Testament. What did you learn about these stories? Why do you think Jude chose these specific stories for his audience?

WATCH

Watch the Week 4 video as a group. Answer the first set of questions on the Week 4 Watch page (p. 83).

DISCUSS

After watching the video, discuss the remaining questions.

Pray together. Pray for the ability to discern false teaching from the truth of the gospel, for the boldness to speak up, and for perseverance in the face of temptation.

Remind everyone to do the personal study pages (pp. 84-101) this week, encouraging them to jot down questions they may have to discuss with the group next week.

_____

_____

_____

_____

WEEK 5

GATHER

Welcome everyone back to the study. Invite girls to ask questions they had from their personal study during the week. Encourage further discussion with the following questions:

- What four elements of nature did Jude use to describe the ungodly teachers?

- How does God's justice better help you understand His love (p. 93)?

- Why do God's words and the examples of God's judgment in the past matter for us today? What influence do they have over how and why we'll contend for the faith?

- How does dissatisfaction in the person of God affect submission to the Word of God? Have you ever been discontent with where God has you or what God has told you and it's led you to "grumble" against Him (p. 96)? Explain.

WATCH

Watch the Week 5 video as a group. Answer the first set of questions on the Week 5 Watch page (p. 103).

DISCUSS

After watching the video, discuss the remaining questions.

Spend some time praying individually for the people you listed on page 101. Then close by praying as a group for those and others in your community you may not yet know by name but need to hear the truth of the gospel.

Remind everyone to do the personal study pages (pp. 104-133) this week, encouraging them to jot down questions they may have to discuss with the group next week.

_____

_____

_____

_____

_____

WEEK 6

GATHER

Welcome everyone back to the study. Invite girls to ask questions they had from their personal study during the week. Encourage further discussion with the following questions:

- Read John 17:20-23. How many times does Jesus pray that Christians may be one? Why do you think He prayed it (p. 107)?

- How have you experienced being built up by praying with other believers (p. 111)?

- Can you think of a time when you shrunk back from sharing a difficult biblical truth in the name of "love"?

Can you think of a time when you were biblically accurate in what you shared but practically loveless in how you shared (pp. 129-130)?

- What does it mean to fear God (p. 131)?

WATCH
Watch the Week 6 video as a group. Answer the first set of questions on the Week 6 Watch page (p. 135).

DISCUSS
After watching the video, discuss the remaining questions.

Pray as a group that you may fear God, have the boldness to speak the truth, and the love to speak it with.

Remind everyone to do the personal study pages (pp. 136-165) this week, encouraging them to jot down questions they may have to discuss with the group next week.

_____

_____

_____

_____

WEEK 7

GATHER
Welcome everyone back to the study. Invite girls to ask questions they had from their personal study during the week. Encourage further discussion with the following questions:

- What kind of person can stand in the presence of God (141)?

- Thinking about all you learned about God from Jude, especially considering all that the gospel has provided for you, what do you think you'd rejoice about while standing in His presence (p. 143)?

- What comes to mind when you think of the word *glory* (p. 152)?

- What does it mean when you say *amen* to Jude's doxology (p. 159)?

WATCH
Watch the Week 7 video as a group. Answer the first set of questions on the Week 7 Watch page (p. 167).

DISCUSS
After watching the video, discuss the remaining questions.

Pray Jude 24-25 aloud as a group to close.

Thank everyone for studying with you and challenge girls to continue contending for the faith. Encourage them to share their personal doxology on social media.

_____

_____

_____

_____

ENDNOTES

WEEK 1

1. John Muir, *Life and Letters in the Ancient Greek World* (New York, NY: Routledge, 2009), 35-36.
2. Jeremy Thompson, *Bible Sense Lexicon: Dataset Documentation* (Bellingham, WA: Faithlife, 2015).
3. Michael J. Wilkins, *The NIV Application Commentary: Matthew* (Grand Rapids, MI: Zondervan, 2004). Retrieved from https://app.wordsearchbible.com, accessed on June 21, 2019.
4. "Definition of Keep," *MerriamWebster.com* https://www.merriam-webster.com/dictionary/keep, accessed on June 21, 2019.
5. Matthew Henry, *Matthew Henry's Concise Commentary on the Whole Bible, Bible Study Tools* https://www.biblestudytools.com/comme ntaries/matthew-henry-concise/romans/5.html, accessed on June 21, 2019.
6. D. A. Carson, *The Gospel According to John* (Grand Rapids, MI: Wm. B. Eerdmans Publishing Company, 1991), 506.

WEEK 2

1. Dick Lucas and Christopher Green, *The Message of 2 Peter and Jude: The Promise of His Coming, The Bible Speaks Today Series* (Downer's Grove: IL, Intervarsity Press Academic, 1995), 172. Retrieved from https://app.wordsearchbible.com, accessed on June 24, 2019.
2. Michael B. Poliakoff, *Combat Sports in the Ancient World: Competition, Violence, and Culture* (New Haven, NJ and London, UK: Yale University Press, 1987), 52-53.
3. "Wrestling Rules at the Ancient Olympic Games" *The Official Olympic Website* https://www.olympic.org/ancient-olympic-games/wrestling, accessed on June 24, 2019.
4. "Definition of Contend," *Bible Hub* https://biblehub.com/greek/75.htm accessed on June 24, 2019.

5. Ibid.
6. J. Ligon Duncan, "Defending the Faith," *First Presbyterian Church* (sermon), May 16, 2004, https://www.fpcjackson.org/resource-library/sermons/defending-the-faith.
7. Ibid.
8. LifeWay Christian Resources, "The 99 Essential Doctrines" *The Gospel Project* (2018) https://www.gospelproject.com/wp-content/uploads/tgp2018/2018/03/99-Essentials-Booklet.pdf, accessed on July 2, 2019.
9. "Definition of Crept in Unnoticed," *Blue Letter Bible* https://www.blueletterbible.org/lang/lexicon/lexicon.cfm?Strongs=G3921&t=ESV, accessed on July 2, 2019.

WEEK 3

1. Ibid, Lucas and Green, 184.
2. Ibid, Lucas and Green, 185. Also from "Definition of Nephilim," *Jewish Virtual Library* https://www.jewishvirtuallibrary.org/nephilim, accessed July 4, 2019.
3. "Definition of Dream," *Blue Letter Bible* https://www.blueletterbible.org/lang/lexicon/lexicon.cfm?Strongs=G1797&t=ESV, accessed on July 4, 2019.
4. "Definition of authority," *Blue Letter Bible* https://www.blueletterbible.org/lang/lexicon/lexicon.cfm?Strongs=G2963&t=ESV, accessed on July 4, 2019.
5. "Definition of Kyrios," *Blue Letter Bible* https://www.blueletterbible.org/lang/lexicon/lexicon.cfm?page=13&strongs=G2962&t=ESV#lexResults, accessed on July 4, 2019.
6. "Definition of Blaspheme," *Bible Hub* https://biblehub.com/greek/987.htm, accessed on July 4, 2019.
7. *The CSB Study Bible* (Nashville, TN: Holman Bible Publishers, 2017), 1984-1985, 2010-2011.
8. "Definition of Instinctively," *Blue Letter Bible* https://www.blueletterbible.org/lang/lexicon/

lexicon.cfm?Strongs=G5447&t=ESV, accessed on July 4, 2019.

9. Ibid, Davids.

10. Ibid, Lucas and Green, 198.

11. Warren W. Wiersbe, *The Wiersbe Bible Commentary: Old Testament* (Colorado Springs, CO: David C. Cook, 2007), 32.

WEEK 4

1. "Definition of Reefs," *Bible Hub* https://biblehub.com/greek/4694.htm, accessed on July 5, 2019.

2. Ibid, Lucas and Green, 204.

3. Scott Sauls "The Compassionate Truth About Judgment" *The Gospel Coalition* (blog), May 20, 2015, https://www.thegospelcoalition.org/article/the-compassionate-truth-about-judgment/, accessed on July 8, 2019.

4. "Definition of Malcontents, Finding Fault" *Bible Hub* https://biblehub.com/greek/3202.htm, accessed on July 7, 2019.

WEEK 5

1. Chart adapted from Peter H. Davids, *The Letters of 2 Peter and Jude: The Pillar New Testament Commentary* (Grand Rapids, MI: Wm. B. Eerdmans Publishing Co., 2006). Retrieved from https://app.wordsearchbible.com, accessed on July 8, 2019.

2. Charles Haddon Spurgeon, "A Weighty Charge," *The Spurgeon Center* (Sermon), March 26, 1876, https://www.spurgeon.org/rsource-library/sermons/a-weighty-charge#flipbook/, accessed on July 9, 2019.

3. "Definition of Mercy" *Blue Letter Bible* https://www.blueletterbible.org/lang/lexicon/lexicon.cfm?Strongs=G1653&t=ESV, accessed on July 10, 2019.

4. John Piper, "What Does It Mean for the Christian to Fear God?" *Ask Pastor John* (podcast), April 1, 2014, https://www.desiringgod.org/interviews/what-does-it-mean-for-the-christian-to-fear-god

5. Ibid.

6. Michael Green, *2 Peter and Jude: An Introduction and Commentary, Tyndale New Testament Commentaries: Volume 18* (Downer's Grove, IL: InterVarsity Press, 1987). Retrieved from https://app.wordsearchbible.com, accessed on July 10, 2019.

WEEK 6

1. Gene L. Green, *Jude and 2 Peter* (Grand Rapids, MI: Baker Academic, 2008), 131.

2. Ibid.

3. "Definition of Present," *Blue Letter Bible* https://www.blueletterbible.org/esv/jde/1/24/t_conc_1167024, accessed on July 12, 2019.

4. "Definition of Blameless," *Blue Letter Bible* https://www.blueletterbible.org/lang/lexicon/lexicon.cfm?Strongs=G299&t=ESV, accessed on July 12, 2019.

5. Ibid, Davids.

6. Augustus M. Toplady "Rock of Ages, Cleft for Me," *Hymnal.net* https://www.hymnal.net/en/hymn/h/1058, accessed on July 15, 2019.

7. "Definition of Majesty" Bible Hub https://biblehub.com/greek/3172.htm, accessed on July 15, 2019, and Lexicon on Jude 1:25, https://biblehub.com/lexicon/jude/1-25.htm, Bible Hub, and Definition of "Megas" https://biblehub.com/greek/3173.htm

8. Walter A. Elwell and Philip W. Comfort, "Definition of Amen," *The Tyndale Bible Dictionary* (Wheaton, IL: Tyndale House Publishers, 2001), 35.

9. "Lexicon for John 3:3" *Bible Hub* https://biblehub.com/lexicon/john/3-3.htm, accessed July 15, 2019.